ARBITRARY BORDERS

Political Boundaries in World History

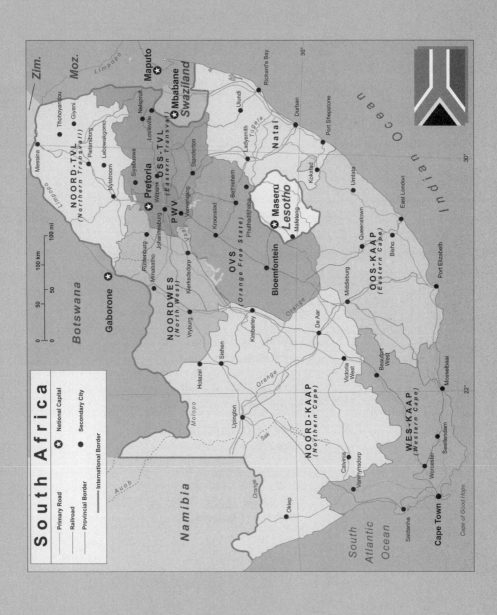

ARBITRARY BORDERS

Political Boundaries in World History

South Africa:
A State of Apartheid

Robert C. Cottrell

Foreword by
Senator George J. Mitchell

Introduction by
James I. Matray
California State University, Chico

CHELSEA HOUSE
P U B L I S H E R S
A Haights Cross Communications Company ®

Philadelphia

FRONTIS Map of South Africa, circa 1997. The country changed configuration through several centuries, finally settling on the borders shown here.

CHELSEA HOUSE PUBLISHERS

VP, NEW PRODUCT DEVELOPMENT Sally Cheney
DIRECTOR OF PRODUCTION Kim Shinners
CREATIVE MANAGER Takeshi Takahashi
MANUFACTURING MANAGER Diann Grasse

Staff for SOUTH AFRICA: A STATE OF APARTHEID

EXECUTIVE EDITOR Lee Marcott
ASSISTANT EDITOR Alexis Browsh
PRODUCTION EDITOR Noelle Nardone
PHOTO EDITOR Sarah Bloom
SERIES DESIGNER Takeshi Takahashi
COVER DESIGNER Keith Trego
LAYOUT EJB Publishing Services

www.chelseahouse.com

First Printing

9 8 7 6 5 4 3 2 1

Library of Congress Cataloging-in-Publication Data
Cottrell, Robert C., 1950-
  South Africa : a state of apartheid / Robert C. Cottrell.
    p. cm. — (Arbitrary borders)
  Includes bibliographical references and index.
  ISBN 0-7910-8257-1 (hardcover)
  1. Apartheid—South Africa—History. 2. South Africa—History. 3. South Africa—Race relations—History. I. Title. II. Series.
  DT1757.C68 2005
  968—dc22
                              2004025349

Dedicated to Stacy and Stefani

Contents

Foreword

Senator **George J. Mitchell**

I spent years working for peace in Northern Ireland and in the Middle East. I also made many visits to the Balkans during the long and violent conflict there.

Each of the three areas is unique; so is each conflict. But there are also some similarities: in each, there are differences over religion, national identity, and territory.

Deep religious differences that lead to murderous hostility are common in human history. Competing aspirations involving national identity are more recent occurrences, but often have been just as deadly.

Territorial disputes—two or more people claiming the same land—are as old as humankind. Almost without exception, such disputes have been a factor in recent conflicts. It is impossible to calculate the extent to which the demand for land—as opposed to religion, national identity, or other factors—figures in the motivation of people caught up in conflict. In my experience it is a substantial factor that has played a role in each of the three conflicts mentioned above.

In Northern Ireland and the Middle East, the location of the border was a major factor in igniting and sustaining the conflict. And it is memorialized in a dramatic and visible way: through the construction of large walls whose purpose is to physically separate the two communities.

In Belfast, the capital and largest city in Northern Ireland, the so-called "Peace Line" cuts through the heart of the city, right across urban streets. Up to thirty feet high in places, topped with barbed wire in others, it is an ugly reminder of the duration and intensity of the conflict.

In the Middle East, as I write these words, the government of Israel has embarked on a huge and controversial effort to construct a security fence roughly along the line that separates Israel from the West Bank.

Having served a tour of duty with the U.S. Army in Berlin, which was once the site of the best known of modern walls, I am skeptical of their long-term value, although they often serve short-term needs. But it cannot be said that such structures represent a new idea. Ancient China built the Great Wall to deter nomadic Mongol tribes from attacking its population.

In much the same way, other early societies established boundaries and fortified them militarily to achieve the goal of self-protection. Borders always have separated people. Indeed, that is their purpose.

This series of books examines the important and timely issue of the significance of arbitrary borders in history. Each volume focuses attention on a territorial division, but the analytical approach is more comprehensive. These studies describe arbitrary borders as places where people interact differently from the way they would if the boundary did not exist. This pattern is especially pronounced where there is no geographic reason for the boundary and no history recognizing its legitimacy. Even though many borders have been defined without legal precision, governments frequently have provided vigorous monitoring and military defense for them.

This series will show how the migration of people and exchange of goods almost always work to undermine the separation that borders seek to maintain. The continuing evolution of a European community provides a contemporary example illustrating this point, most obviously with the adoption of a single currency. Moreover, even former Soviet bloc nations have eliminated barriers to economic and political integration.

Globalization has emerged as one of the most powerful forces in international affairs during the twenty-first century. Not only have markets for the exchange of goods and services become genuinely worldwide, but instant communication and sharing of information have shattered old barriers separating people. Some scholars even argue that globalization has made the entire concept of a territorial nation-state irrelevant. Although the assertion is certainly premature and probably wrong, it highlights the importance of recognizing how borders often have reflected and affirmed the cultural, ethnic, or linguistic perimeters that define a people or a country.

Since the Cold War ended, competition over resources or a variety of interests threaten boundaries more than ever, resulting in contentious interaction, conflict, adaptation, and intermixture. How people define their borders is also a factor in determining how events develop in the surrounding region. This series will provide detailed descriptions of selected arbitrary borders in history with the objective of providing insights on how artificial boundaries separating people will influence international affairs during the next century.

Senator George J. Mitchell
October 2003

Introduction

James I. Matray
California State University, Chico

Throughout history, borders have separated people. Scholars have devoted considerable attention to assessing the significance and impact of territorial boundaries on the course of human history, explaining how they often have been sources of controversy and conflict. In the modern age, the rise of nation-states in Europe created the need for governments to negotiate treaties to confirm boundary lines that periodically changed as a consequence of wars and revolutions. European expansion in the nineteenth century imposed new borders on Africa and Asia. Many native peoples viewed these boundaries as arbitrary and, after independence, continued to contest their legitimacy. At the end of both world wars in the twentieth century, world leaders drew artificial and impermanent lines separating assorted people around the globe. Borders certainly are among the most important factors that have influenced the development of world affairs.

Chelsea House Publishers decided to publish a collection of books looking at arbitrary borders in history in response to the revival of the nuclear crisis in North Korea in October 2002. Recent tensions on the Korean peninsula are a direct consequence of Korea's partition at the 38th parallel at the end of World War II. Other nations in human history have suffered because of similar artificial divisions that have been the result of either international or domestic factors and often a combination of both. In the case of Korea, the United States and the Soviet Union decided in August 1945 to divide the country into two zones of military occupation ostensibly to facilitate the surrender of Japanese forces. However, a political contest was then underway inside Korea to determine the future of the nation after forty years of Japanese colonial rule. The Cold War then created two Koreas with sharply contrasting political, social, and economic systems that symbolized an ideological split among the Korean people. Borders separate people, but rarely prevent their economic, political, social, and cultural interaction. But in Korea, an artificial border has existed since 1945 as a nearly impenetrable barrier precluding meaningful contact between two portions of the same population. Ultimately, two authentic Koreas emerged, exposing how an arbitrary boundary can create circumstances resulting even in the permanent division of a homogeneous people in a historically united land.

Korea's experience in dealing with artificial division may well be unique, but it is not without historical parallels. The first set of books in this series on arbitrary boundaries will provide description and analysis of the division of the Middle East after World War I, the Iron Curtain in Central Europe during the Cold War, the United States-Mexico border, the 17th parallel in Vietnam, and the Mason-Dixon Line. A second set of books will address the Great Wall in China, the Green Line in Israel, and the 38th parallel and demilitarized zone in Korea. Finally, there will be volumes describing how discord over artificial borders in the Louisiana Territory, Northern Ireland, and Czechoslovakia reflected fundamental disputes about sovereignty, religion, and ethnicity. Admittedly, there are many significant differences between these boundaries, but these books will strive to cover as many common themes as possible. In so doing, each will help readers conceptualize how complex factors such as colonialism, culture, and economics determine the nature of contact between people along these borders. Although globalization has emerged as a powerful force working against the creation and maintenance of lines separating people, boundaries likely will endure as factors having a persistent influence on world events. This series of books will provide insights about the impact of arbitrary borders on human history and how such borders continue to shape the modern world.

James I. Matray
Chico, California
April 2004

1

The Sharpeville Massacre

In the early afternoon of March 21, 1960, South African police fired on a large crowd of demonstrators who were challenging the government's practice of apartheid, or racial segregation, in the southern Transvaal town of Sharpeville. When the shooting subsided, 69 black Africans were dead and between 180 and 300 were left injured. That same day, and over the course of the following three weeks, other confrontations resulted in additional casualties as well as mounting anger on the part of numerous Africans. Indeed, the Sharpeville Massacre helped to ignite the armed resistance that many members of the Pan Africanist Congress (PAC) and the African National Congress (ANC) came to support. That in turn convinced the government to ban both the PAC and the ANC and to hand out life prison sentences to many African leaders, including attorney Nelson Mandela.

The bloodletting undoubtedly occurred because of the arbitrary, racially drawn borders that had systematically enveloped South African society by early 1960 but that had long characterized the continent's southernmost sector. While increasingly many nonwhites were becoming unwilling to accept segregation and racial discrimination, many white residents of South Africa proved equally determined to retain the preferential treatment apartheid afforded them. All of this occurred during the Cold War era (following World War II), when the world's greatest powers, the United States and the Soviet Union, felt compelled to respond to the growing demands for national sovereignty emanating from Africa and the rest of the underdeveloped world.

From 1957 to 1975, 45 independent African countries discarded the arbitrary borders associated with colonialism, including those involving territorial boundaries, political subjugation, and racial barriers. Influenced by the currents of nationalism and anti-imperialism unleashed by World War II, this floodtide of new states emerged because of the discrediting of racist stereotypes and the insistence of Africans that they be afforded autonomy. In various locations, the transfer of power proceeded smoothly, accompanied by goodwill and great expectations that were frequently quickly dashed.

Although relatively poor, many of the new nations were wealthier than India, which was often considered a model for countries in the so-called Third (or underdeveloped) World. Moreover, African leaders like Ghana's Kwame Nkrumah and Tanzania's Julius Nyerere fervently believed in the potency of "Africanness" and a shared destiny. As Nyerere indicated, "Africans all over the continent, without a word being spoken … looked at the European, looked at one another, and knew that in relation to the European they were one."[1] They were as one in demanding an end to long-standing arbitrary borders of an imperial, racial, and cultural cast. The story of South Africa particularly demonstrates the illusory nature of permanent white dominance confronting the reality of inevitable majority rule by nonwhites.

From the advent of Dutch imperialism along the Cape of Good Hope in the mid-seventeenth century, European colonists erected social, political, and economic barriers of an arbitrary quality that discriminated against indigenous peoples. Following the British takeover of the Cape Colony in the early nineteenth century, descendants of the original Dutch settlers, called the Boertrekkers, or Boers, migrated into other sectors of southern Africa and were soon joined by large numbers of German and English immigrants. In the new communities they created, the Boers established racially rigid social orders of an arbitrary nature.

With the passage of time, new immigrants from India and eastern Africa added to the already diverse racial makeup of the inhabitants of southern Africa while encountering the kind of color-based prejudice that Africans did. So too did the so-called Coloreds, who resulted from miscegenation (the intermingling) of white, blacks, and others.

A series of wars against both African tribes and English troops concluded with British control, but white supremacist ideas and practices remained in place. That continued following the establishment of the Union of South Africa in 1910, with a further hardening of racial barriers once the National Party, which championed apartheid, came to power in 1948.

By 1960, separation of the races characterized South African society, in keeping with a large number of parliamentary acts upholding the distinctly arbitrary practice of apartheid. Various white liberals and radicals opposed the black–white divide, as did many nonwhites, who formed various organizations condemning the system's inequities. These included the ANC, the South African Indian Congress, and the more militant PAC. While the ANC and the South African Indian Congress sought change through legislative pressure and nonviolent action, including civil disobedience, the PAC adopted a more aggressive stance.

On March 21, 1960, the combustible combination of apartheid, longstanding grievances, and PAC agitation spawned large demonstrations, involving over 20,000 participants, in the Transvaal. These resulted from the increasing frustration that PAC members felt regarding the ANC's purported failure to establish its own political program. The PAC insisted that Africans begin employing "positive action" to create a new society. This led to the PAC's "status campaign," announced in August 1959, which called for the conducting of economic boycotts—something Africans had long resorted to—until black customers were treated in a nondiscriminatory fashion.[2] The PAC hoped to persuade the masses that they, acting collectively, could achieve liberation on their own rather than relying on legal approaches dependent on white allies. The campaign, PAC members believed, could help overcome a deeply rooted sense of racial inferiority.

However, Ghanaian leaders, who were well-regarded by the PAC, dissuaded its members from continuing this protest. Thus, the PAC adopted instead a new tack, the "positive action campaign," intended to condemn the "pass laws," which sought to control the very movement of blacks.[3] Long employed by both the Dutch and the British, pass laws became more notorious still as the system of apartheid emerged, with Africans 16 years of age and older required to display a pass or so-called reference book whenever asked to do so by the police or government officials. Strikingly too, the government established special commissioners' courts to ensure that the pass laws were enforced. The PAC now resorted to its positive action campaign in an attempt to convince employers to pressure the government to discard the pass laws.

A series of events, including the attainment of independence by Ghana and Guinea, along with guerrilla warfare in Kenya, evidently convinced the PAC that the timing was propitious for more radical moves. A visit to South Africa by British prime minister Harold Macmillan contributed to this view. Speaking to parliament on February 3, 1960, about the "Winds of Change," after having traveled through the continent, Macmillan referred to

> the awakening of national consciousness in peoples who have for centuries lived in dependence upon some other power. Fifteen years ago this movement swept through Asia....Today the same thing is happening in Africa. The most striking of all the impressions I have formed since I left London a month ago is the strength of this national consciousness. The wind of change is blowing through the continent. Whether we like it or not, this growth of national consciousness is a political fact. We must all accept it as a fact. Our national policies must take account of it.[4]

South African prime minister Hendrik F. Verwoerd immediately defended his apartheid regime.

Robert Mangaliso Sobukwe and other PAC leaders traveled around South Africa intimating that the organization was about to initiate a direct action campaign challenging apartheid. They passed out thousands of leaflets, urging that people not show up for work and instead join in the protest campaign. Those same materials exhorted blacks to remain nonviolent. In the early morning hours of March 21, 1960, only 10 days before a similar action was scheduled by the ANC, members of the PAC knocked on doors throughout Sharpeville to awaken inhabitants, hoping to encourage them to participate in a series of protests. A number of individuals readily went along, while others felt pressured to do so. At the same time, the PAC urged bus drivers to stay away from their jobs to ensure that buses would be unavailable to transport laborers. Consequently, many, relying on bicycles or walking, headed for work, but soon encountered organizers, who made various threats "to burn their passes or to 'lay hands on them,' if they failed to turn back."[5]

Ambrose Reeves, the bishop of Johannesburg, later indicated that the PAC appeared to lack a firm plan of action, with many blacks simply milling about. Various PAC figures, including Sobukwe, did show up at police stations in the Transvaal, intending to turn in their passes and expecting to be arrested. More important, word soon spread that a significant statement regarding passes was about to be made by the chief Bantu commissioner at the police station. By eight o'clock on the morning of March 21, blacks congregated there, soon joined by another group that had been gathering in Seeiso Street. Waiting patiently, the crowd eventually grew to 5,000–20,000 people, depending on which estimate is to believed. Reeves has indicated that he believes individuals showed up for different reasons, with some determined to protest pass laws, others coerced into appearing, and still others simply wishing to find out what would be said. Apparently, the police neither queried why so many had congregated nor ordered the crowd to depart.

At around 10 o'clock, aircraft began flying overhead, sometimes diving right above the gathered throng, evidently with the expectation that such action would cause the crowd to disperse. Instead, children shouted, "Hoorah! Hoorah!" while the sight of the planes only induced the size of the crowd to further swell.[6] Finally, Nyakale Tsolo, a leader of the PAC in Sharpeville, heard from the police that a top government official would arrive in the early afternoon. Some in the crowd chose to depart, at least for the time being, heading into cafes or returning home to listen to radio coverage of the events.

Many returned shortly after lunch, Reeves reports, "in a

Reenactment of the Sharpeville massacre. More than 50 demonstrators protesting the 1960 Sharpeville massacre were killed when police opened fire on a crowd on May 16, 1964. The 1960 shootings took place when nervous police opened fire into a large crowd that had descended on the Sharpeville police station in response to the Pan Africanist Congress (PAC) call for a strike to protest the system of passes used by the white government to enforce apartheid.

happy mood. Very few Africans had gone to work, and an idle, holiday atmosphere pervaded the town."[7] Songs rang out, along with various slogans, such as "Afrika!"[8] Photographs of the crowd, which largely included women and children, indicated that those gathered appeared to be unarmed, although a few wielded sticks. Both news photographers and the location superintendent indicated as much, noting the amicable manner in which they were greeted. The crowd continued to grow, as did the number of police at the station. The police moved about freely, sporting rifles on their shoulders, smoking, and talking to one another. As time passed, PAC leaders urged those in attendance to avoid damaging the fence around the police station.

Eventually, Lieutenant Colonel Pienaar showed up, having

been informed that "a most dangerous situation" existed. Pienaar mistakenly believed that police at the station had earlier been forced to employ a baton charge, tear gas, and gunshots to disperse the crowd. He too failed to ask those outside the station why they had gathered. By this point, he had 300 men to call on, but reasoned that a baton charge would not suffice. Later, Pienaar insisted that he had been unable to order the crowd to disperse: "I did not have any time to do that. I would have liked to." Instead, within 15 minutes of his arrival at the scene, he ordered his men to line up. They faced the crowd, which was situated on the western and southern sides of the police station. To the north stood three Saracen tanks. Soon, Pienaar told his men, "Load five rounds," hoping this would intimidate the crowd.[9] A number of the policemen boasted weapons that already held many more rounds than Pienaar had told them to load. They perhaps were remembering recent events in nearby Cato Manor, where a liquor raid had led to the killing of nine policemen.

The next sequence of events is difficult to pinpoint precisely, with some witnesses reporting that shots rang out and others indicating that a policeman first instructed his colleagues to "fire."[10] At some point, nevertheless, shots hurtled into the crowd, which, in a panicked state, began fleeing. Hospital records noted that the vast majority of those injured were shot from the back, many falling near the western fence or in the field located to the north and northeast of the police station. However, one woman was found on the ground a good distance from the fence. Another was hit as she was shopping in a grocery store, and a third woman was shot while in her backyard. Those shootings occurred as policemen fired from the tops of the Saracens.

Altogether, the police continued targeting individuals for at least 40 seconds, sending out 705 rounds, despite the fact that Pienaar insisted he issued no order to fire. Later, the police indicated they heard shots from the crowd, which was rushing the fence and through the double gate, and hurling stones at them.

Victims included children, women, and older men, with head

and stomach injuries common and various individuals badly mutilated. The vast majority of casualties involved onlookers who were simply trying to find out what was taking place at the police station. Some of the wounded suffered the additional indignity of being taunted by those who had shot them. At times they were ordered to leave the area, while those who attempted to help them were also ordered away. The Reverend Robert Maja of the Presbyterian Church, who raced to assist those injured by the police fire, later testified that many appeared stunned by the events that had unfolded.

Other demonstrations occurred on March 21 in Langa and Cape Town, while the presence of Sabre jets effectively scattered a crowd of 20,000 in Evaton. For the next three weeks, a series of massive strikes and demonstrations by blacks took place, all condemning the Sharpeville massacre. Altogether, thousands of men and women were arrested, while Black Monday—as the massacre came to be called—and the days that followed culminated in police actions leading to scores of deaths and hundreds of injured black Africans. The police in a township like Sharpeville obviously viewed a crowd of Africans with trepidation and as a mob that had to be dealt with by force. Evidently, the police in Sharpeville, who expected blacks to defer to them, considered the thousands who had gathered at the police station as a rebellious mob that had to be quashed.

The Sharpeville events resulted in government restrictions on public assembly and moves to ban major black organizations, such as the ANC and the PAC, thus demonstrating a resort to long-standing arbitrary borders of a political nature. This occurred as the strikes and demonstrations continued to condemn the police violence on March 21 and apartheid in general. The government declared a state of emergency and published emergency regulations, allowing local officials to forbid political gatherings and to arrest and detain individuals deemed a threat to the public safety. Over the course of the next several months, the South African regime, relying on the emergency provisions, arrested 12,000 nonwhites, including many black leaders, such as

ANC president Albert Luthuli and other top figures in the ANC, the PAC, and the Indian National Congress.

The Sharpeville massacre and the heightening of repressive measures resulted in worldwide condemnation. The United Nations Security Council called for South Africa to terminate apartheid and its heavy-handed treatment of nonwhites. Indeed, as Frank Welsh indicates, "Sharpeville began to establish South Africa as internationally untouchable."[11] Indeed, Welsh likened what happened in Sharpeville on March 21, 1960, to events that had occurred in India in 1919, when British soldiers killed 379 men, women, and children in the Punjabi city of Amritsar. He also compared Sharpeville with the killing of four students at Ohio's Kent State University in 1970, or the murder two years later, on "Bloody Sunday," of 13 civilians in Londonderry, Northern Ireland.

Shortly following the massacre, ANC and the PAC leaders both opted to head underground and to initiate military resistance against South Africa's apartheid government and the racially restrictive arbitrary borders that it championed. Sobukwe later indicated that Sharpeville enabled Africans to surmount their fear of violating colonial edicts. Subsequently, "it became respectable to go to jail and emerge as what Kwame Nkrumah called 'Prison Graduates.' We stripped the white man of that weapon against us."[12] Allister Sparks refers to Sharpeville as "the turning point" at which black activists "switched from strategies of nonviolence to those of guerrilla strategy. When what had been a civil-rights campaign turned into a civil war of sorts." This occurred as the South African government added to its legacy of apartheid legislation by producing "a torrent of security legislation ... and South Africa started becoming a police state." Soon, "violence met violence in an escalating spiral."[13]

The arbitrary borders long devised by white segregationists were thus lengthened, eventually producing a corresponding response on the part of black nationalists. Those borders, drawn during the course of over 300 years of oppression and subjugation, involved territorial, economic, social, and racial restraints of an often rigid cast. From early colonial times through the advent of the Cold War, whites in South Africa strove to maintain hegemony over nonwhites as fully as possible, eventually opting for a wholesale legal system of segregation. By the end of the 1950s, nonwhites, influenced by challenges to colonialism sweeping across the African continent and throughout the underdeveloped world, contested that very dominance through a variety of means, including the employment of direct action techniques. The massacre that occurred at Sharpeville in March 1960 only deepened hostilities on both sides of a political and racial conflict that threatened to tear South Africa apart. Ultimately, arbitrary borders appeared to lack permanence, or at least this was true of those based on notions of supposed racial inferiority and supremacy—corrosive ideas that continued to tragically separate humankind in the modern era.

2

Early South African History

Early in time, arbitrary borders of a geographic, racial, or cultural nature remained very much in flux in southern Africa, as new peoples and social arrangements—including, eventually, kingdoms—appeared. Approximately three-and-a-half million years ago, the species *Australopithecus africanus* first arrived in southern Africa. Between 1 million and 90,000 B.C., *Homo erectus* resided in the region, making use of fire and stones. The San hunter-gatherers spread across southern Africa by 15,000 B.C., eventually encountering the Khoikhoi cattle- and sheepherders, who had moved from the area today known as Botswana. Both the San and the Khoikhoi possessed yellowish or copper-hued skin. White settlers later referred to the San as Bushmen and called the Khoikhoi Hottentots.

By 300 A.D., brown-skinned people had migrated south of the Limpopo River, speaking Bantu languages and residing in chiefdoms, where they farmed. Eventually, the San, Khoikhoi, and Bantu peoples all hunted and gathered plant food, with the San and the Khoikhoi (the two groups were eventually referred to as the Khoisan) also searching for shellfish.

Through the early stages of the fourteenth century, South African communities were concentrated in the northern and eastern plains, although the Khoisan soon controlled the southern and southwestern Cape territory. Sotho-Tswana speakers settled throughout the high veld (open grassland country) interior, while Nguni-speaking peoples resided along the southeastern coast.

In 1487, Portuguese sailors led by Bartolomeu Dias, who was seeking a passage to India, reportedly became the first Europeans to encounter South Africa. Ten years later, Vasco da Gama guided another Portuguese expedition around the Cape on the way to India. During the next century, more Portuguese ships undertook the odyssey, as Portugal conducted a slave trade to the Western Hemisphere but only skirted into South Africa. Subsequently, Dutch, French, English, and Scandinavian crewmen also sailed past the Cape to Asia.

When the initial European settlers came to the Cape, the

Khoisan population stood at about 50,000, with regularly occurring seasonal migrations. Early in the seventeenth century, the English attempted to rely on convicts to help settle the Cape, but the effort proved unsuccessful. Then, in 1652, Jan van Riebeeck and 80 employees of the Dutch East India Company arrived in Table Bay, located at the Cape's northern end, to construct a fort and provide Dutch ships with foodstuffs. The establishment of a Dutch outpost soon reshaped South Africa's arbitrary borders, and did so in tragic fashion.

Initially, the Dutch planned to establish only a trading post, but they quickly decided to take over land held by the Khoisan, relying on superior weaponry. Van Riebeeck reported that his men had taken away thousands of head of cattle from "the Hottentots," and predicted the capture of "many savages … without resistance … to be sent as slaves to India, as they still always come to us unarmed."[14] Soon fearing the loss of their grazing lands, the Khoisan began battling the Dutch, but proved unable to penetrate the fortress that ultimately shielded the Europeans.

Constructing a base at the site eventually known as Cape Town, the Dutch East India Company, then the world's largest trading corporation, afforded some of its former employees status as free burghers (middle-class individuals). The company also began to import slaves to toil on farms, while providing several one-time employees with twenty-acre plots. As the Dutch operations expanded into the interior, thus recasting territorial borders, local farmers suffered accordingly.

More settlers—most of whom were Dutch Calvinists but many others were Germans—arrived, with settlement at first taking place on the Cape peninsula. In 1679, the Dutch East India Company began awarding free passage to South Africa and grants to land well beyond Table Bay. Among the newer immigrants were Huguenots who had originally left France for the Netherlands to escape religious intolerance. By the early stages of the eighteenth century, the white farmers, who no longer worked for the Dutch East India Company, referred to themselves as

In the late 1400s, several Portuguese trading expeditions sought passage to India around the Cape of Good Hope. None of these groups stopped long enough to settle the area, but they paved the way for the Dutch East India Company, which sent Jan van Riebeeck and a crew of 80 to establish a Dutch fort in 1652. The fort eventually became an outpost and changed the course of events in South Africa.

"Afrikaners," to set themselves apart from the company's employees, called "Europeans." Company officials deemed themselves as socially more desirable than the whites who had headed into the interior, terming themselves "Kaapenaar."[15]

Consequently, cultural and racial arbitrary barriers emerged, separating Afrikaners and Europeans. The obvious feelings of superiority that the Dutch colonists possessed were similar to those exemplified by other European imperialists in dealing with nonwhite peoples around the globe. Such sensibilities apparently justified, in the minds of Europeans, the takeover of native lands and the subjugation of native peoples. This also resulted in arbitrary borders intended to underscore the primacy of the colonial power.

White sheep- and cattle ranchers took over arable land encircling Cape Town as the local population declined because of smallpox and violent acts committed by the Dutch. The loss of livestock crippled the Khoikhoi, whose fragile political system crumbled. Khoikhoi now tended the sheep and cattle held by the Afrikaners and, notwithstanding their nominal independence, increasingly made up a subordinate caste. Lacking immunity to smallpox, the Khoikhoi experienced demographic setbacks, with their society all but disintegrating. At the same time, the number of actual slaves in the colony mounted, with a few coming from Mozambique but many more arriving from Madagascar, Indonesia, India, and Ceylon. Within a century-and-a-half, approximately 60,000 slaves resided in the colony.

In Cape Town, intermarriage between settlers and Khoisan was hardly infrequent, although it seldom involved those situated at the top of the political, social, or economic hierarchy that characterized colonial life. Nevertheless, one scholar indicates that intermarriage was "surprisingly frequent and socially acceptable" before the close of the eighteenth century.[16] Still, racially drawn arbitrary borders appeared to have been present since the beginning of the colony.

At different points, the Khoisan continued to resist the persistent Dutch expansion, conducting extended guerrilla warfare in which farms were attacked, livestock herded away, and farmers killed. On occasion, the San drove out Afrikaner farmers from large plots of land, but retribution tended to be swift and merciless, with hundreds of San murdered and their children gathered up as slaves. Indeed, the survivors of the countless battles that broke out between Europeans and the Khoisan were driven into indentured servitude or slavery, eventually commingling with imported slaves. Over half of the burghers held slaves, but few claimed ownership of as large numbers as in the New World since South Africa initially remained free of the kinds of plantations that cropped up across the Atlantic Ocean during this era.

By the close of the eighteenth century, however, large estates had appeared, containing many servants, Khoikhoi, and slaves. A highly stratified racial order of an arbitrary nature increasingly characterized the colony, with whites located at the apex, slaves and Khoikhoi situated at the bottom, and a small number of free blacks adopting a precarious middle position.

Slaves possessed no right to marry, to attend to the needs of their children, to hold property, or to draft legal documents. Female slaves were forced to engage in heavy physical labor and to prostitute themselves to garner money for the Dutch East India Company. The ever-present threat of violence, which often was acted upon, sustained the institution of slavery while inducing many slaves to escape. Some managed to link up with native groups, while various bands attempted to survive by stealing from settler homesteads. A small number of slaves achieved their freedom through the process of manumission (the voluntary freeing of slaves), which generally was allowed only for those held in bondage who had been baptized and who possessed apparent means of support. In addition, more Asian slaves, several of whom were skilled artisans, were freed than Madagascan or African ones, who tended to toil in the fields. However, South African slaves and mulattoes were favored too. Women appeared far more inclined to liberate their slaves than did men.

Free blacks tended to congregate in Cape Town, getting by "as artisans, cooks, innkeepers, fishermen, and small-scale retail traders," according to Leonard Thompson.[17] Government edicts attempted to restrict the very attire of free black women, to prevent them from adopting styles favored by European colonists.

During the eighteenth century, small bands of burghers drove past the Olifants River, becoming the first Trekboers—seemingly self-sufficient farmers who opposed government control in the

Nomadic Khoikhoi tribesmen taste porridge as it heats in a cauldron, circa 1882. The Khoikhoi, descendants of both the San and the Bantu, are with those groups referred to as Khoisan. The Dutch, having established their outpost in 1652, quickly set about taking over land held by the Khoikhoi and other tribes, stealing livestock and enslaving the tribespeople.

face of harsh frontier existence. Tensions arose between Cape officials and the Trekboers, who contested efforts to tax them, require military service, or restrict their use of land. The advance of the Trekboers, pushing back territorial arbitrary borders, continued nevertheless, with a northward movement toward the Orange River and eastward to the arid territory of the Great Karoo and the Little Karoo.

Cape Town authorities did attempt to establish administrative posts in the frontier lands, but distance and temperament ensured that the Trekboers would heavily influence government operations. The Trekboers often operated at a near-subsistence level, hardly becoming immersed in market developments. Schools, which were only sporadically found throughout the colony, were nonexistent in the lands occupied by the Trekboers.

The skewed sex ratio of the frontier areas led to more miscegenation, although little intermarriage eventuated, resulting in a growing "bastaard population" made up of the offspring of these mixed unions.[18]

During the 1730s, the Khoisan conducted extended guerrilla campaigns against the settlers, while in the 1770s, additional clashes occurred as colonial farmers drove deeper into lands occupied by the Khoisan. Armed militia or commandos fought against the Khoisan, sweeping up women and children who were forced into indentured labor. Settlers mandated the wielding of passes by the children of Khoikhoi slaves or Khoikhoi parents. By 1779, encroachments by white settlers resulted in the first of a series of frontier wars with the Xhosa, a Sotho-Tswana people who resided west of the Great Fish River.

In 1795, the British, through an expedition led by General Sir James Craig and Admiral Lord George Keith Elphinstone, took control of both the Cape and a broad swath of largely uninhabited territory, reaching west of the Fish River and south of the Gariep. As war with Napoleon Bonaparte appeared increasingly likely, the British government was troubled by the fact that French ships increasingly stopped at the Cape before heading to India. With the Dutch East India Company suffering liquidation, the British decided to temporarily hold the colony for the beleaguered Dutch monarchy of the Prince of Orange.

Cape Town stood as the sole port of entry into the area and the lone city. The entire colony consisted of "25,000 slaves, 20,000 white colonialists, 15,000 Khoisan and 1,000 freed black slaves."[19] Robert Ross indicates that in the north, colonial society's "most advanced representatives," eventually referred to as Griquas or Oorlams, possessed partial Khoisan origins, used the Dutch language, and considered Christianity a means to affirm their status.[20]

The first British takeover proved short-lived, lasting only until 1803, when the Treaty of Amiens restored Dutch rule. The last few years of the initial British rule were hardly uneventful, characterized by a rebellion that broke out in 1799 involving

Khoisan who had already been subjugated by Trekboers. This effort involved an attempt on the part of the insurgents to retake the "country of which our fathers have been despoiled."[21]

Because of the Napoleonic Wars, British officials reestablished control, abolishing the slave trade in 1808 and moving forcefully against the Xhosa in the area west of the Zuurveld region. In 1814, the Dutch formally ceded the colony, solidifying arbitrary borders in southern Africa of an imperial nature. Moreover, like the Dutch, the British proved determined to maintain white dominance in the region.

At no point were South Africans, whether white or black, consulted by the British on matters of colonial rule. Moreover, within a few years, British administration had reshaped the central government of the Cape, local governments, land policies, and the general settlement of the territory. In 1820, 5,000 British settlers arrived, quickly heading for frontier areas, with most arriving in the Zuurveld region, alongside the Great Fish River. The Cape government hoped that the new settlers would serve as "a buffer against advancing Xhosa populations," as John Reader indicates.[22] For these settlers, as for the Trekboers earlier, frontier existence proved arduous, with recurrent crop difficulties and attacks on their livestock by Xhosas. Receiving little assistance from the Cape government, the settlers formed militia to protect their homesteads and families; they also continued to resent the government in Cape Town. Many quickly abandoned farming altogether, moving into towns such as Grahamstown, soon South Africa's second largest.

Tensions between the Trekboers and Cape Town heightened thanks to a series of legal and social reforms adopted by the British authorities and because of the growing number of British settlers. Mercantile interests were significant as well, including capitalistic economic practices based on free labor. In 1826, shortly following a slave insurrection, the Colonial Office attempted to regulate working conditions for slaves, in addition to restricting physical punishment, encouraging religious education, sponsoring Christian marriage, and affording them legal rights, including enabling slaves to purchase their freedom. In 1828, the settlers supported passage of Ordinance 50, granting legal equality to the Khoisan and free blacks.

In spite of this action, feelings of racial superiority hardly dissipated. They continued notwithstanding the abolition of slavery in 1834, which was nevertheless paired with a required four-year period of apprenticeship that amounted to bondage, resulting in the retention of indentured labor. Many former slaves continued to work on farms, with the 1841 Master and Servant Ordinance regulating labor contracts and supposedly placing nonwhite South Africans on an equal legal footing with Europeans. In actuality, that measure instituted criminal sanctions for purported acts of "disobedience, defiance and resistance" if workers violated contractual agreements.[23] Thus, South Africa continued to possess racially rooted arbitrary borders even as slavery was discarded.

Along with the eradication of slavery, the mounting number of settlers also markedly reshaped the relationship between the colony and Africans situated "beyond its border," Robert Ross states. Initially, the larger number of Xhosa allowed for a standoff against the militarily superior colonists, with neither capable of sustaining lengthy campaigns. Furthermore, the frontier (or arbitrary border) separating the colony and other Africans remained "imprecisely defined, both spatially and socially."[24] However, after the British military entered the fray, the rough parity largely ended as the soldiers crushed the Xhosa, impoverishing them, destroying their fields and homes, and scattering their livestock. Continual reinforcement of English troops thwarted any temporary successes by the Xhosa, as did a readiness to mete out terrible punishment, including the beheading and mutilation in 1835 of the Xhosa ruler, Hintsa, who had demonstrated a willingness to conduct peace negotiations. Various settlers in the colony's eastern sector actually benefited from the conflicts, with lands opened up for settlement and supplies required for British soldiers.

Thus, through the first third of the nineteenth century,

European colonization in South Africa proved disruptive to the indigenous peoples, who quickly encountered unprecedented arbitrary borders of all kinds. These ranged from newly shaped territorial boundaries, through which white settlers pushed aside the Khoisan, Xhosa, and other dark-skinned Africans, to racial and class hierarchies that placed Europeans at the apex of social, political, and economic orders. Given the miscegenation that invariably occurred in South Africa, the racial boundaries

CAPE TOWN

For centuries prior to European colonization, the Khoisan occupied the Table Bay region from which Cape Town, originally called De Kaap and then Kaapstad, emerged. In 1652, the Dutch East India Company established a trading outpost to serve Dutch sailors skirting around the Cape of Good Hope on their way to the East Indies. Gradually, the number of European inhabitants increased, while the Khoisan were displaced or subjugated. The Dutch commander, Jan van Riebeeck, introduced slavery, with most of those held in bondage coming from eastern Africa or Asia.

The prominence of Cape Town, the earliest permanent settlement by Europeans in South Africa, continued to heighten, as it served first the Dutch and later the British military headquarters. Under British rule, greater attempts were undertaken to strengthen administrative control of the territories, something that resulted in a good deal of resentment and considerable resistance, particularly on the part of the Trekboers. Cape Town officials also had to contend with continued clashes that pitted settlers, whether Dutch or British, against indigenous groups like the Xhosa. Those frontier clashes involved determined efforts on the part of white settlers to extend the colony's arbitrary borders and by the native peoples to resist encroachments on their land.

Back in Cape Town, a diverse population emerged, reaching the 16,500 mark by 1806. Nearly 10,000 of those inhabitants were slaves, while 800 free blacks resided there as well. Following the termination of the slave trade in 1808, the percentage of slaves in Cape Town diminished while British immigration increased. By 1840, British immigrants made up the dominant ethnic group in Cape Town and were determined to solidify their own artificially constructed racial, cultural, and political barriers.

sometimes appeared fluid, but from the beginning, colonial society acquired a rigidity that suppressed nonwhites. This proved true even though slavery, early practiced by the Dutch, was soon discarded by the British. Nevertheless, whites remained determined to retain the preferential treatment that had characterized their stay in South Africa. To ensure that was so, they soon resorted to new arbitrary boundaries of both a geographic and racial cast.

3

The Great Treks

English rule proved unsettling to both European and non-white populations in South Africa, eventually resulting in massive, historic odysseys. As a consequence, the territorial makeup (or geographical arbitrary borders) of the colony were reshaped, as were those of the Zulu nation situated along South Africa's eastern coast. Ultimately, a *difaqane* or *mfeqane* (translated as "clubbing," "crushing," "scattering," or "time of emptiness") spewed forth in southern Africa.[25]

During the early stages of the nineteenth century, Dingiswayo, chief of the Mthethwa, and his commander, Shaka, guided Zulu warriors against the Ndwandwe along the Mhlatuse River, located in northern Nguni territory. Shaka then succeeded Dingiswayo, who was slain by his foes, and molded the new Zulu kingdom into a militaristic, centralized state dominating the inhabitants of northern Nguni.

Conducting a reign of terror, Shaka eliminated entire tribes and enslaved others, leading many to withdraw before the onslaught. Those fleeing, in turn, often displaced still others, who engaged in a similar exodus. This sequence of events rippled across southern Africa, enabling the Sotho, the Swazi, and the Ndebele to flourish, while also allowing the Pedi and the Tswana to expand their boundaries.

At the same time, the desertion of pasture lands, the appearance of groups of refugees, and reports of atrocities helped to shape the attitudes of the Boers, who undertook the own migration into the interior of southern Africa. Called the Great Trek, this procession of white farmers took them into the territories later known as the Transvaal and the Orange Free State—lands with distinct political and racial arbitrary borders. This chapter will examine both of these migrations and their effect on each other.

By the end of the eighteenth century, a pair of northern Nguni tribes, the Mthethwa and the Ndwande, had become the most powerful in the territory, located south of the Phongolo River, making up the region later called KwaZulu. The two tribes possessed linguistic and cultural patterns similar to those of the

Xhosa, who were situated 800 hundred miles away on land that contained Dutch and English settlers. Undergoing considerable transformations, the Mthethwa and the Ndwande discarded the earlier practice of absorbing defeated tribes into their communities, treating them instead as subjugated forces. Centralized rule over large expanses of territory characterized their governance.

In 1816, Zwide, chief of the Ndwandwe, and Dingiswayo, chief of the Mthethwa, readied for a showdown. Dingiswayo had long relied on coercive diplomacy to hold sway over larger numbers of subjects, with Shaka, who initially had guided only some 2,000–3,000 Zulu, serving as his top commander. In 1817, Zwide bested Dingiswayo, who was replaced as head of the Mthethwa by Shaka. Three years later, Shaka crushed Zwide, becoming the dominant non-European figure in southern Africa.

Shaka discarded long-held traditions, negating individual family control over marriages, institutionalizing terror, and intensifying the scope of warfare. At the same time, Shaka initiated "the formation of what can only be called a nation," with distinct arbitrary borders.[26] By 1828, the Zulu controlled 18,000 square miles of land from Drakensberg to the Indian Ocean, with defeated tribes scattering widely. Possibly as many as 100,000 people were subject to Shaka's rule, which ended in 1828 when his half-brothers assassinated him.

Fleeing to Delagoa Bay, Soshangane, who had been one of Zwide's military chieftains, conducted campaigns similar to Shaka's, eventually ruling a swath of land that reached to the sea from the Zambezi. Another Ndwandwe military leader, Zwangendaba, held sway over the area that makes up present-day Malawi and Tanzania. Mzilikazi, Zwide's grandson, was pushed across the Vaal River, where his men took control of land but also suffered attacks by Zulus; by Griquas, as the Baastards came to be called; and by Boers, in the midst of their own Great Trek. Eventually, Mzilikazi's followers ended up in the territory that later became Zimbabwe. Another chief, Sobhuza, who had earlier fled from Zwide, moved into the region that came to be called Swaziland.

Then there were refugees who supported the Sotho leader Moshoeshoe, who established Basutoland, later known as Lesotho. That state adopted a policy of tolerance toward opponents and sought to survive through peaceful approaches, with no standing army. Moshoeshoe declared, "Peace is like the rain which makes the grass grow, while war is like the wind which dries it up."[27]

The sweep of indigenous armies proved cataclysmic for southern Africa, which witnessed arbitrary borders rise and fall. As historian Frank Welsh notes, European chroniclers referred to extended travels across a wasteland that amounted to killing fields, complete with "the scattered bones of the dead."[28] Some survivors resorted to cannibalism. Traditional indigenous cultures and societies crumbled, with warlords demanding that those left behind either join with them or endure the possibility that their very survival might be called into question. Below the Drakensberg, Nguni tribes fared somewhat better, deferring to Zulu domination or moving south of the Tukela River to avoid confrontation. Zululand itself featured absolute rule, with outlying areas having been largely depopulated, especially in the territory that became Natal, south of the Tukela.

Refugees continued fleeing southward, encountering the Xhosa, who were experiencing population pressures of their own. Moving ahead of Zwide and Shaka, Matiwane, a Ngwane chief, tore through Natal, Basutoland, and the Cape, conducting his own bloody march that continued for ten years before the Thembu halted his sweep. Subsequently, the Thembu and the neighboring Mpondo were able to establish viable communities, keeping the Xhosa apart from the Zulu. The Mpondo, led by chief Faku, welcomed thousands of Mfengu refugees from Natal. Guided by aggressive chiefs, the *bhaca* (homeless ones) seemingly got along with the Thembu and the Mpondo.

Such coexistence was encouraged by Western missionaries who reached out to both refugees and the warlords associated with the mfeqane. The evangelist George Schmidt of the Moravian Brotherhood had established the first mission at

Genadendal in 1737, but it possessed only limited appeal for the Khoikhoi. The missionaries departed in 1744, with another crop returning near the end of the century. The London Missionary Society (LMS) desired to offer "the Glorious Gospel of the Blessed God to the heathen."[29] In 1799, the first members of the LMS arrived, soon clashing with government officials regarding the treatment of slaves and indigenous peoples. Eventually, other Protestant missionaries arrived, including additional British ones, along with Germans and French Huguenots.

During the first decades of the nineteenth century, the Cape became, quite possibly "the most heavily missionized area in the world," according to Robert Ross.[30] The climate proved conducive to Europeans, colonial society allowed missionaries to thrive there, and the early missions largely succeeded, affording protection for the Khoisan against labor exploitation. In addition, the missionaries seemingly offered a new vision for people whose social order had been torn apart by colonization. Evangelical ideals helped to bring about changes pertaining to working conditions and slavery itself in the Cape colony.

That development, along with the devastation wreaked by the tribal wars and general frustration regarding British colonial policies, served as spurs for another mass exodus, the Great Trek by white Afrikaners or Voortrekkers (Dutch for pioneers) that began unfolding by the mid-1830s and eventually involved approximately 15,000 people.

War on the colony's eastern frontier during 1834 and 1835 had destroyed a considerable number of farmhouses. One of the Voortrekker leaders, Piet Retief, indicated that migration was necessary to "allow us to govern ourselves without ... interference in future" from the British government. He continued: "We are resolved, wherever we go, that we will uphold the just principles of liberty; but, whilst we will take care that no one shall be held in a state of slavery, it is our determination to maintain such regulations as may suppress crime, and preserve proper relations between master and servant."[31] Thus, Retief considered it necessary for his fellow Voortrekkers to shape their own political, cultural, and racial arbitrary borders.

The Great Trek involved movement northward into the territories later comprising the Transvaal, Natal, and the Orange Free State. Initial excursions led to reports that a great amount of fertile, largely unpopulated land was available in Natal and on the high veld or central open grasslands beyond the Orange River. Massive migration began in 1836, with the Voortrekkers ignoring early warnings from Mzilikazi, the Ndebele chief who attacked several camps. The Voortrekkers responded by circling their wagons and calling on their guns to withstand the Ndebele assaults. Soon, the Voortrekkers formed a partnership with the Griqua, the Korana, and previously displaced Tswana to fight off the Ndebele. New Voortrekker emigrants arrived, allowing for more offensive operations. Withdrawing from southern Transvaal, Mzilikazi headed to Zimbabwe's southwestern sector.

Divisions arose among the Voortrekkers, who were led by Andries Hendrik Potgieter, Gerrit Maritz, Piet Uys, and Retief. Potgieter's followers remained on the high veld, but most of the Voortrekkers headed for the more fertile Natal, moving across the Drakensberg, the dragoon mountain range that separated the high veld from the South African coast. Initially, the Great Trek's participants had formed a republic at Thaba 'Nchu, located close to present-day Bloemfontein, but as sectarianism developed, Retief, Maritz, and Uys all led their followers to Natal. Potgieter, by contrast, proceeded northward to construct the republic of Winburg, situated on terrain that is now part of Free State, and the republic of Potchefstroom. Eventually, however, he traversed the Vaal River to establish the Transvaal, which took up the region presently making up Gauteng and Northern Province, along with a portion of North–West Province. Potgieter carved out amicable relations with his black neighbors, who remained more fearful of Mzilikazi's Ndebele or sporadic expeditions by the Korannak, Khoikhoi pastoralists who had resided north and south of the middle Orange River.

Retief attempted to rely on diplomacy with both the British

A monument constructed in Pretoria to the Great Trek of 1838. Both Europeans and nonwhite indigenous people alike were unhappy with British rule of South Africa, which resulted in the mass exodus of several groups of people into the interior of the country. The Great Trek brought the Boers inland to the Transvaal and the Orange Free State. Pretoria, established as capital of South Africa in 1855, is located within the Transvaal and was named after Andries Pretorius, a Voortrekker who settled the area.

and Dingane, but the Zulu king, in early February 1838, struck at Retief's party, killing hundreds of Voortrekkers and servants, and taking tens of thousands of livestock animals.

Setbacks continued for several months, but reinforcements at the end of the year strengthened Retief's position. In mid-December, a massive Zulu army began attacking the Voortrekkers, but following Pretorius's arrival, the Zulus suffered around 3,000 casualties at the battle of Ncome, or Blood River, while the settlers experienced no fatalities. The Zulu kingdom splintered, with Mpande, Dingane's brother, choosing to align with the Voortrekkers, ensuring the king's defeat. The Voortrekkers' victory enabled them to continue taking hold of more pastureland, soon leading to their claim to most of the fertile territory situated between the Tugela and the Mzimkhulu rivers.

The Voortrekkers' presence in Natal disturbed British officials, and General Sir George Napier, the colonial governor, determined that the land the settlers claimed had to be annexed or declared independent. The British noted that the Voortrekkers were invading nations ruled by blacks, but also worried that other European powers or the United States might seek to establish settlements along South Africa's eastern shores. The earlier march by Shaka had led to the demise or dispersal of scores of African tribes that had recently occupied Natal. Now, vast expanses of land, including those first encountered by the Voortrekkers, appeared uninhabited. However, concerns remained regarding how the settlers would treat the indigenous people, a number that had surged from about 10,000 to five times that amount, following the defeat of Dingane.

The Voortrekkers established the Republic of Natal, devising a constitution in March 1839 that called for a representative democracy featuring the Volksraad, a 24-person council, chosen annually through open ballots cast by adult white males. The Volksraad admitted representatives from the high veld communities, while the government emerged as something of a federal republic.

In September 1840, the Volksraad, possessing legislative, executive, and judicial powers, wrote to Napier, seeking independence for Natal. Four months later, the Voortrekker representatives sought to firm up an alliance with the Cape, promising in turn to avoid slave trafficking, to refrain from attacking neighboring peoples without informing British officials, and to accord equal rights to British citizens. Just when it appeared that such a proposal might prove acceptable, the Republic of Natal extended its territorial demands southward to both the Mmzimkulu and the Mzimvubu Rivers, thereby infringing on lands held by indigenous peoples whose independence was recognized by the British.

For some time, British officials had opposed extending the reach of their South African colony and the scale of its arbitrary borders, being content with the present size of the empire, the unrivaled potency of the British navy, and the dominance of British commerce. Shortly after the Voortrekker migration commenced, however, British officials increasingly worried that the settlers could destabilize South Africa's eastern frontier. Consequently, in 1842, British forces took control of the harbor of Durban, while the next year, British officials decided to incorporate the region into the British Empire. Influenced by evangelicals, a British special commissioner assured "that there shall not be in the eye of the law any distinction of colour, origin, race, or creed; but that the protection of the law, in letter and in substance, shall be extended impartially to all alike."[32]

Some Voortrekkers remained in Natal, but the bulk of them, led by Potgieter and refusing to accede to British rule, headed back across the Drakensberg to the high veld. The settlers in Potchefstroom and Winburg formed a new state, complete with its own agenda, which included support for farming and the exclusion of nonwhites. Voortrekkers continued to prefer loose governance only, as did Potgieter, soon to depart for Andries-Ohrigstadt, some 300 miles northward. Another schism quickly arose, pitting Potgieter's followers against those of Jacobus Burger, a leader of the Volksraad, whose backers apparently desired more democratic governance. Finally, Potgieter chose to depart yet again, heading up north for Zoutpansberg, where he helped to form a patriarchal society. Another Voortrekker leader, Andries Pretorius, ended up in Potchefstroom, where he battled against British claims to the Orange River territory, a move opposed by the Volksraad in Ohrigstadt, by Potgieter, and by many Voortrekker (now called Boer) farmers situated to the south.

Increasingly spread out, the Boers confronted all sorts of difficulties, including some related to the landscape itself. Potgieter's followers hoped to establish commercial relations outside their colony, relying on the Portuguese settlement situated at Delagoa Bay. However, the lowland terrain they resided on attracted disease-carrying mosquitoes and flies, taxing both the Boers and their livestock. The settlers believed that their earlier triumph over Mzilikazi's Ndebele entitled them to the high veld, but Sotho and Tswana tribes began returning to the region. Also dwelling on the open grassland country were white farmers who retained allegiance to the Cape, and Griquas, pastoralists of both Khoikhoi and mixed descent. Each of these groups, in turn, experienced internal divisions, tensions that were heightened by the activities of various European missionary groups, including the London Missionary Society, the Paris Evangelical Society, and the Wesleyan Missionary Society.

Great Britain became more and more involved as a result of attempts by colonial administrators to stabilize the arbitrary borders at the northern frontier by forming client states, which included East Griqua, led by Adam Kok, and Lesotho, headed by Moshoeshoe. Then, in 1848, Sir Harry Smith, governor of the Cape colony, annexed Xhosa land between the Keiskamma and the Kei rivers, and claimed British control of the full territory located between the Orange and the Vaal rivers, purportedly to safeguard the rights of native chiefs, Queen Victoria's rule, and her subjects. This region came to be called the Orange River Sovereignty, and boasted many Boers and most of Lesotho.

Deferring to Smith's preemptive action and responding to demands by emigrants and missionaries, the British government led by Major Henry Warden, also constructed "new internal boundaries" of an arbitrary nature that sought to separate less powerful African chiefdoms from those of Moshoeshoe.[33] However, the British suffered a military defeat at Viervoet, in 1851, at the hands of Moshoeshoe's Basotho. The British responded by retreating from the high veld, recalling Smith, and negotiating with Pretorius, which resulted in the awarding of independence to Boers residing in the area north of the Vaal River.

After attempting to wreak vengeance against Moshoeshoe, which caused determined resistance, the new British commander withdrew his forces. Subsequently, a special commissioner agreed in early 1854 to turn over governance of the territory to Boers. Thus, the Boers, through the Bloemfontein and Sand River agreements, achieved their long-desired independence in both the Transvaal and the Orange Free State.

As a result of these two Great Treks—one characterized by shifting groups of indigenous peoples and the other involving white settlers—the arbitrary borders that nations and the world's greatest colonial power had drawn in southern Africa were significantly reshaped. Mass migrations of human beings, resulting from incessant warfare and the determination to remain free from imperial dictates, dramatically altered existing social, economic, and political fabrics. Entire societies and tribes were torn apart, great numbers of refugees were created, and open land was made available for settlement.

With alliances changing as frequently as did territorial designs, small numbers of powerful chiefs aligned with or battled against growing numbers of white settlers, mainly the Trekboers, Afrikaners who sought to break away from the Cape and who came to be known as the Boers. While divisions arose among the Boers themselves, most of the white settlers were united in wishing to remain apart from British control. That determination, coupled with the difficulty of administering vast expanses of territory far removed from colonial centers, led to the British decision to grant independence to the settlers.

However, the devising of these new arbitrary borders neither resolved the dilemmas that the newly independent Boers had to contend with, nor shaded the persistently watchful eye of British imperial authorities.

4

Natal and the Boer Republics

Near the midpoint of the nineteenth century, British colonial operatives chose to deal with portions of southern Africa in different manners, causing the region's arbitrary borders to remain in flux. The British retained control of the southernmost areas, including Natal, but allowed white Afrikaners to establish the Orange Free State and the South African Republic (the Transvaal state). With the passage of time, however, British colonial leaders viewed those states less favorably, particularly because of the repeated encroachments made by the Boers on African nations and tribes—which threatened wholesale warfare—and the Boers' competing demands for control of the area's rich mineral resources, including diamonds. Eventually, the British adopted a more aggressive strategy toward the Boer republics, again threatening to alter the area's arbitrary borders and the very existence of those new nation–states.

Seeking to prevent another imperial power from making inroads along the southernmost coast of Africa, and concerned about the Voortrekkers' treatment of slaves, Great Britain decided to annex Natal. The actual announcement of the British takeover did not occur for more than two years, taking place in August 1845, as a largely impotent Volksraad continuing to meet until Lieutenant-Governor Martin West arrived in Natal in December. Almost immediately, colonial officials turned aside the Voortrekker policy of relocating African settlements and rejected many Voortrekker land claims. As a result, several Voortrekker families joined together and attempted to establish their own independent republic in the Klip River district ruled by Mpande. However, other Voortrekkers chose to remain in Natal, including a number of merchants and farmers.

In 1848, the colony's governor, Sir Harry Smith, met with the Boer leaders of the would-be republic and promised to cede almost two million acres of land to several hundred Voortrekker families, hoping to convince them to remain part of Natal. British officials in London, however, refused to allow open-ended ownership of land; this convinced most of the remaining

Boer families to depart, causing about 40 percent of Natal's territory to wind up in the hands of speculators.

Following the exodus by most Boers, a land scheme triggered by the adventurer Joseph Byrne attracted some 5,000 immigrants—most of whom were middle-class individuals from England and Scotland, but others arrived from Germany and Mauritius—between 1849 and 1852. Many, however, quickly determined that their landholdings were too sparse and either returned home, headed for the high veld, or chose to live in towns, influencing places like the inland capital of Pietermaritzburg and the port town of Durban. As late as the mid-1850s, fewer than 10,000 whites lived in Natal, compared with more than 100,000 Africans, who, having lost their chiefs, tended to be fragmented. Nevertheless, the whites remained determined to maintain hegemony by solidifying political and racial borders of an arbitrary nature.

Indeed, both colonial officials and missionaries sought to cement relationships with indigenous peoples—an effort that also involved the question of arbitrary borders but not simply ones of a territorial nature. The Cape's borders remained chaotic, but Natal's proved "defined and peaceable," with the Mpondo and Mpande's Zulu to the south and north respectively posing no real threat to the settlers.[34]

In Natal, writes Timothy Keegan, a pattern of white rule developed in which many Africans were forced to contend with "a homestead economy." Keegan continues:

> Here the essential instruments of coercion and control, which would later be elaborated elsewhere in southern Africa, were first developed. And it was here too, earlier than elsewhere, that there first developed the parasitic relationship between a colonial society and its black suppliers of peasant produce, and between white absentee landowners and rent-paying African homesteads.[35]

Helping to shape colonial policy in Natal, particularly pertaining to indigenous peoples, was Theophilus Shepstone, the son of a Wesleyan missionary. Shepstone remained a key figure in the region for over three decades, beginning in the mid-1840s. Lieutenant-Governor West named Shepstone to a land commission, which sought to reshape land policy. Under the Voortrekkers, the Republic of Natal had granted all of the land to whites. Shepstone contended that "equality meant deprivation" for blacks in Natal, as would the failure to enable them to maintain their traditional legal practices.[36] Along with the other commissioners, Shepstone pinpointed a series of locations, on some two million acres, to be reserved for black inhabitants; this approach proposed new arbitrary borders for Africans, deliberately isolating them from other residents of southern Africa. Support from missionaries and the inhabitants' own determination enabled these communities, or reserves, to succeed for a time.

However, white colonists bitterly opposed the system of reserves, insisting that blacks be afforded only sufficient land to eke out a minimal level of subsistence. That, in turn, whites believed, would compel blacks to work for them for nominal amounts. In addition, the British government itself was hardly enthralled with the reserves, failing to allocate much financial assistance. The colonial governor, Harry Smith, appointed another land commission, which contended that a mere 250,000 acres of land, or perhaps even 100,000, would suffice for the reserves and avoid encouraging the Africans' supposed "habitual indolence."[37]

Following West's untimely death in 1849, Benjamin Chilley Pine became the new first lieutenant-general in Natal and agreed that the reserves were too extensive and should be divided, with their population compelled to serve on white farms. However, opposition from missionaries and Shepstone prevented the adoption of Pine's call for a reduction of the reserves.

Backed by the Colonial Office and Pine's successor, John Scott, Shepstone acquired almost unchecked power in Natal. He defended blacks against whites, but he did so in a paternalistic fashion. He actually favored the removal of most of Natal's

Africans beyond its borders, which would have alleviated pressure involving black settlement. He sought to take hold of No-Man's-Land to the south and Basutoland (southern Sotho), adjacent to Natal, but to no avail. Ultimately, Shepstone devised a system, soon to be repeated, in which blacks were led by their chiefs, who in turn were subject to British approval, and had to follow traditional native law on communally owned territory. Certain individuals who were deemed properly qualified could seek permission to dwell under British law, through which they could acquire the right to vote. Eventually, Shepstone believed, majority rule would result as a consequence of this arrangement, but exemptions proved difficult to obtain as white settlers bitterly opposed the possibility of the black majority running the government. These settlers envisioned a day when whites might be compelled to depart from southern Africa altogether rather than accede to black-dominated rule.

Recent studies have called into question Shepstone's reputation for having shielded blacks against white exploitation, with some scholars pointing to how he welcomed laborers from Zululand and other northern sectors. In addition, the government admitted Indian immigrants, mostly low-caste Hindus from Madras, including many women. These Indians, who began arriving in 1860, were obligated to fulfill contractual terms of five years' labor. When their period of low-paid indentured servitude ended, they could begin a similar labor stint, purchase their freedom, or return to India.

During the same period in which Shepstone helped to shape colonial policy governing both the Voortrekkers and blacks, the Orange Free State and the South African Republic came into existence. The treaty resulting from the Bloemfontein Convention of February 1854 acknowledged the independence of the Boers, who were residing between the Orange and Vaal rivers. The Free State constitution established a unicameral Volksraad for the republic, allowed for a chief executive to be elected by adult white males who had registered for military service, called for equality before the law, and championed freedom of the press. White farmers dominated the new state, infringing on the territory of the Griquas, located in the south. War erupted in 1858, pitting Boer farmers against Moshoeshoe's Sotho over the fertile terrain in the Caledon River valley. Seven years later, tensions arose again as whites sought to make deeper inroads into the region.

For a brief period during the previous decade, the possibility existed that the Orange Free State might be joined with the Transvaal to produce a lone republic. In 1853, Martinus Wessel Pretorius replaced his father as the top commandant, and pushed for the unified approach, which would again redraw arbitrary borders. President Johannes Hoffman of the Orange Free State and President Jacobus Boshof of Transvaal strongly opposed that possibility. Boshof, in fact, believed that reunion with the economically successful Cape colony made far more sense. The Cape governor, Sir George Grey, proved amenable to such a notion, reasoning that the separation had been a disastrous mistake. To Grey, only Great Britain could rule over the diverse white-dominated states, but imperial officials proved unwilling to take on that task, refusing at that point to again reshape South Africa's arbitrary borders.

Even Pretorius's attainment of the presidency of both republics in early 1860 failed to link the Orange Free State and the Transvaal, where the political situation remained in flux. At the same time, the physical boundaries of the Transvaal proved to be generally fixed, involving the Limpopo River and its tributaries to the north and the Vaal to the south. The Lembotho mountains shaped the western perimeter, beyond which lay Portuguese Mozambique. These boundaries, as Frank Welsh indicates, offered "another, invisible, line, that of the westward limit of the tsetse fly, the carrier of sleeping sickness."[38] Farming was impracticable in that region, which was characterized by hunting instead.

One observer explained how dealings with indigenous peoples shaped arbitrary borders along the frontier.

> [We are asked to] consider the danger of the Frontier. There
> may be some danger, but gentlemen seem to amass large for-
> tunes in a very short time up there in spite of the danger. Our
> sympathies have been appealed to—honorable members have
> drawn such a dreadful picture of barbarism rushing into the
> country, and laying everything waste with fire and sword. But
> in the same breath we are told that the value of farms is
> increasing at an enormous rate.[39]

Thus, the white settlers proved determined to hold vast expanses
of territory, which required devising arbitrary borders that benefited Voortrekkers at the expense of Africans.

In the Transvaal, small groups of Voortrekkers proved antagonistic to one another, proving incapable of addressing economic
or military problems. With the Transvaal Volksraad failing to
meet at all at one point during the mid-1850s, a *kommissieraad*
resulted, which allowed Volksraad representatives within a particular area to effectively operate for the full parliament. Religious
differences added to the schisms, with calls to establish an independent Voortrekker church and to separate from the Cape
colony—a proposal supported by the Volksraad but opposed by
Lydenburg, the settlement founded in 1850, whose residents
formed their own representative assembly. War threatened to
break out between the rival Voortrekker factions, but a compromise was reached by 1858, resulting in a new constitution, the
Rustenburg Grondwet, which called for an elected president, an
executive council, and a unicameral Volksraad selected by white
voters. In September 1859, the representative body of the South
African Republic convened in Pretoria (named after Andries
Pretorius) for its first session. Three months later, the new state
incorporated the Lydenburg and Utrecht Volkraads.

The following year witnessed Pretorius's taking of power in
both the Orange Free State and the South African Republic. The
action by Pretorius occurred despite admonitions by Grey that
such a move would violate the agreements allowing for the creation of the new states. The Transvaal Volksraad responded to

Early twentieth-century black, Chinese, and white South African gold miners. Diamond and gold mine owners maintained strict racial standards, exploiting cheap black labor for dangerous, physical, unskilled tasks but assigning whites as overseers and machinery operators. In the towns that sprang up around the mines, blacks could only reside in segregated areas.

the warning by suspending Pretorius, thereby initiating a series of moves that eventually convinced Paul Kruger, a member of the Krygsraad, to institute martial law. Eventually, negotiations led to a presidential election in 1864 that returned Pretorius to power.

Pretorius's presidency witnessed numerous clashes with African chiefdoms who were troubled by the Boers' obvious determination to expand their territorial reach. The Orange Free State achieved favorable terms of settlement following an 1865 war with the Basotho, then still headed by Moshoeshoe. In 1868, the British high commissioner, Sir Philip Wodehouse, annexed the country of the Basotho, which whites called Basutoland.

As the 1860s neared a close, the Boer republics appeared increasingly stable, with territorial issues apparently resolved and confrontations with African states suppressed. At the same time, the Boers themselves remained determinedly independent, continued to sparsely occupy the lands they claimed, possessed no industry, and failed to establish a strong agricultural base. However, the discovery of diamonds close to Kimberly, 550 miles from Cape Town, altered perceptions about the Orange Free South and the South African Republic.

The initial discovery of diamonds occurred on terrain held by the Griquas but claimed by both the Boer republics. Work intensified at the Kimberly mine, soon the richest in the world. Thousands of European immigrants, Cape and Natal speculators, Afrikaner farmers, and black workers poured into the area. Initially, boom towns appeared that largely ignored prevailing policies of racial segregation. This greatly troubled the Boers, who were already disturbed that their republics were not benefiting from the diamond explorations. The British annexed the land, called Griqualand West, in 1871.

The development of labor relations in the diamond fields influenced the course of future race relations and hence arbitrary borders in South Africa. As Leonard Thompson noted, "White populism created a color bar in Kimberly."[40] By 1872, a diggers' committee, featuring whites alone, established rules intended to maintain South African racial standards. The committee sought to preclude black diggers and to place other strict controls on black laborers, who would endure body searches without warrants and suffer physical punishment for retaining diamonds for which they held no title. A strict racial hierarchy developed in the mining industry, with skilled European immigrants operating machines; black Africans performing dangerous, physical labor; and white South Africans overseeing black laborers.

With the passage of time, mining towns adopted racially restrictive policies too, with only whites allowed to dwell there with their families. Blacks could reside only in segregated sections of town or in all-male compounds located next to the mines. Furthermore, during the 1870s employees had to carry passes in Griqualand West, with independent blacks compelled to present passes indicating that they were exempt from the pass laws. Various white diggers desired still more in the form of arbitrary borders, however, calling for an independent republic, connected to the Orange Free State, that would keep blacks in their place.

5

Annexation
and Revolt

The move to annex Griqualand West demonstrated a growing determination by British officials to adopt a more aggressive approach toward major portions of the African subcontinent. That process intensified during the last three decades of the nineteenth century, resulting in the takeover of "Basutoland, Griqualand West, the South African Republic, the Transkei and Bechuanaland."[41] In addition, the British took control of territories previously controlled by the Zulu and the Pedi. Setbacks occurred too, with the British suffering defeats at the hands of the Zulu and being temporarily driven from the Transvaal. In 1900, British hegemony returned to both the Transvaal and the Orange Free State, which became the Orange River County. As these developments transpired, the region's arbitrary borders— geographic, political, and racial—altered course repeatedly, demonstrating the indeterminate nature of such boundaries. Much of this occurred at the same time European imperial powers continued to lay claims over larger portions of Africa.

By the 1870s, the Boers, then dwelling in the Orange Free State and the South African Republic, struggled to uphold the Christianity and literacy they were supposedly transmitting to portions of southern Africa, often in the face of disconcerting odds. As John Reader indicates, the Boers, with their pool of capital diminishing, resorted to barter while become "increasingly impoverished." They failed to train either ministers or teachers from within their own ranks. As a result, one chronicler indicated that their children were

> growing up with less care bestowed upon them than upon the beasts of the field—without the ability to read or write even their mother tongue, without any instruction in the knowledge of a God that made them, having at their command no language but a limited vocabulary of semi-Dutch, semi-Hottentot words....[42]

All the while, the Boers retained the determined independence that had initially induced them to break away from the Cape colony.

That very determination confronted the ever-present obstacles involved in creating viable states in southern Africa's interior, the same terrain whose mineral resources—particularly diamonds and gold—attracted greater European, African, and British imperial interests. This helped to convince the British Colonial Office to reestablish control over the region—something that the Boers would oppose—ultimately resulting in major conflagrations. Other factors seemingly were at work as well, including humanitarian concerns about the treatment of Africans by the Boer republics.

The last half of the nineteenth century and the early stages of the twentieth century comprised an age of empire-building, with European powers wrestling for control over various regions around the world, including Africa, which experienced incursions by the Belgians, French, Germans, Italians, Portuguese, and Spanish, as well as by the British. Those powers dramatically remade the continent's arbitrary borders. At a bare minimum, the British were intent on protecting their important naval base at Simonstown, close to Cape Town, and on maintaining their sea route to Asia.

Also during this period, complaints arrived at the Colonial Office, then under the direction of Lord Carnarvon (Henry Howard Molyneux Herbert), that the pass laws enacted by the South African Republic prevented workers from easily reaching the mining fields or farms and plantations in the Cape and Natal. This demonstrated how arbitrary borders of a racial nature could ironically work against the very economic interests of the groups that purportedly benefited from those rigidly drawn barriers. A perception arose that a takeover of the high veld would safeguard the interests of both the empire and settlers in regard to African workers. Indeed, Carnarvon envisioned a federation that would include the Cape colony, Natal, and the Boer republics, all contained within the British empire.

Theophilus Shepstone, secretary for native affairs in Natal in 1874–1878, called for the reassertion of British rule over the Boer republics, a move that Carnarvon also supported. By this point, the South African Republic was all but bankrupt. Backed by Natal settlers, Shepstone tracked developments at the diamond mines and reports of gold deposits in the eastern sector of the Transvaal. Like diamond mine operators, he also recognized that the government of the South African Republic was competing for migrant labor. While Lord Carnarvon remained strongly adverse to slavery and forced labor of any sort, he recognized that British interests in the regions required a sufficient pool of wage workers. With these factors influencing colonial officials, the British prevented the Boer republics from taking control of the diamond fields and then moved in 1877 to annex the tottering Transvaal.

After the empire annexed Griqualand West, the colony's Thlapling inhabitants experienced the steady loss of grazing land to miners, land speculators, and colonial operatives. In 1878, a revolt ensued, perpetrated by Thlapling chiefs and Griqua and San fighters. Following the British quashing of the rebellion, the Thlapling suffered the loss of cattle, relocation to rural areas, and onerous taxation. Other battles broke out pitting British and colonial forces against the Xhosa, the Pedi (in eastern Transvaal), the Zulu, and the Sotho, with only the latter able to hold out against British attacks. Consequently, the British terminated "the economic and political independence of southern Africa's two most powerful black states," the Pedi and the Zulu, even though British soldiers did suffer a terrible setback at Isandlwana in 1879, at the hands of Zulu warriors.[43]

Nevertheless, the visions of a federation came to naught, as did hopes for a steady pool of migrant labor. A rebellion led by Paul Kruger commenced in the Transvaal in 1880, resulting in the first Anglo-Boer War (labeled the War of Independence by Afrikaners). In December 1880, the Transvaal Volksraad issued the Proclamation of Pardekraal, demanding the restoration of independence. That document allowed for boundary disputes to be resolved through arbitration and agreed that policies pertaining to indigenous peoples would be determined "after deliberation with the Colonies and States of South Africa."[44] At the same time, the Transvaal Boers experienced martial law and brief clashes with British forces. During the most significant of these, the British suffered 93 casualties, the Boers but 1. Among the British fatalities was Sir George Colley, high commissioner and governor of the Transvaal and Natal.

The humiliating British defeat led to a cease-fire and the setting up of a royal commission that met with Kruger to determine the fate of the South African Republic. The Convention of Pretoria, delivered on August 3, 1881, accorded "complete self-government, subject to the suzerainty [supremacy] of Her Majesty," to the Transvaalers. This placed "control of external relations ... and the conduct of diplomatic intercourse with foreign powers" in the hands of British officials, to the dismay of the Volksraad.[45]

Notwithstanding such consternation, Kruger became president of the South African Republic in 1883. Along with other representatives of the reestablished sovereign state, Kruger soon left for London, seeking to revise the Convention of Pretoria, including provisions involving boundaries and suzerainty. British officials agreed to discard suzerainty regarding the South African Republic in most instances and to reduce that state's indebtedness, while Kruger accepted a newly drawn western border that "kept the Road to the North open."[46] That border remained unsettled, with Kruger choosing to provisionally annex additional territory until compelled to back down by the British government. Still, the Boer established firm control over the Transvaal, with attacks against "the Ndebele in the east, the Rolong Tswana in the west, and the Venda of the Soutpansberg in the north."[47]

As these developments occurred, Afrikaner nationalism surged, along with resentment toward British influence in the area. In addition, the newly acquired riches provided the Transvaal republic with the possible means "to escape from the British suzerainty it unwillingly accepted," says J.M. Roberts.[48] At the same time, the discovery of a large reef of gold in the Witwatersrand, the hilly ridge around Johannesburg in the

South African Republic, threatened to again transform relationships with Great Britain. Thousands of miners and speculators, both white and black, poured into the Transvaal, turning Johannesburg into a major urban center and making the South African Republic the wealthiest in the region. A number of individuals, including Cecil Rhodes, Alfred Beit, and Barney Barnato, who had acquired great wealth through the Kimberly mines, now invested heavily in the Rand (the new name for Witwatersrand). Workers moved in from Kimberly, but many European immigrants, along with individuals residing in the coastal colonies, arrived as well. Soon, the Rand contained the world's largest gold-mining operations. There, corporations rather than individual prospectors increasingly became involved in mining and gold extraction.

As had occurred in Kimberly, the gold-mining industry adopted racially restrictive labor policies. Determined to reduce labor costs, mining companies relied on easily exploited black labor while again compelling those workers to dwell in all-male compounds and paying them one-eighth the amount received by white miners, who also had subsidized housing.

The government of the South African Republic also responded quite differently to various groups of workers, setting "color bars for particular mining tasks," while "ruthlessly" crushing black laborers who had revolted.[49] In 1895, the Volksraad in the South African Republic devised a pass law, crafted by mine operators, granting them even greater control over their workers. Africans could be imprisoned for neglecting to carry appropriate work passes.

The Kimberly and Rand mining districts provided precedents for future labor policies—or arbitrary borders involving workers and employers—on the continent. Rules and regulations intended to provide a guaranteed pool of cheap labor were carved out to restrict Afrikans' freedom of movement. Such practices never involved "*employment* in the sense of a relationship which was mutually beneficial to the employer and the employee, but always the *exploitation* of an indispensable

A statue of Cecil Rhodes by Sir Hamo Thornycroft. Son of a Hertfordshire clergyman, Rhodes (1853–1902) was to make most of his fortune in the Kimberly diamond mines, which opened in 1871. A trip through the Transvaal and Bechuanaland territories in 1875 convinced Rhodes that the British should rule all of southern Africa (the statue shows Rhodes facing north, toward unconquered lands, with a map of Africa in his hand). Rhodes became prime minister of Cape Colony in 1890. After orchestrating a failed coup d'etat, he moved to Rhodesia (named in his honor; now Zimbabwe). He died in South Africa and is buried in Zimbabwe.

resource," John Reader points out. Employers viewed the rural, uneducated, and black workers "as a race apart, with aptitudes and aspirations quite different from those of Europeans and unlikely ever to change." Recruiters reasoned that wage increases would hardly affect "the native standard of living," and would only result in such workers toiling for a briefer period, thereby hindering industrial growth.[50]

During the 1890s, the British undertook concerted efforts to challenge the Boer monopoly on gold-mining operations in the South African Republic. Indeed, gold from the region helped ensure London's standing as the world's preeminent financial capital. However, President Kruger and the South African Republic possessed other interests, seeking to benefit the Afrikaner farmers, not outside financiers. To the chagrin of the latter, Kruger's tax and customs policies presented no incentives for additional development in the Transvaal. An inevitable confrontation resulted, with the English mining magnate and Cape prime minister Cecil Rhodes seeking to overthrow the government of the South African Republic.

Along with the British government, Rhodes had already prevented that state from expanding its boundaries. In 1885, the British prevented the South African Republic from driving westward by naming Bechuanaland, later known as Botswana, a protectorate. Four years later, Rhodes's own British South Africa Company obtained a charter enabling it to establish broad rights in a region located north of the Limpopo. In 1891, shortly after becoming prime minister, Rhodes had men from his company move past the Limpopo to stake a claim to territory that eventually made up first Rhodesia and then Zimbabwe. Kruger, for his part, attempted to accomplish what Hendrik Potgieter had sought: an independent path to the Indian Ocean. In 1895, the South African Republic took control of Swaziland, while British officials annexed the land between Zululand and Portuguese Mozambique. Consequently, the potential for conflict remained between the South African Republic and the British empire.

Nevertheless, the Transvaal regime appeared to have broken "the British stranglehold," having established its own commercial routes through Mozambique via the Delagoa Bay railroad.[51] Of significance too, the South African Republic carved out diplomatic relations with Germany, which in 1892 had annexed South West Africa.

Back in England, political leaders focused on the Transvaal, with its Witwatersrand gold deposits. The new secretary of state for the colonies, Joseph Chamberlain, was a determined imperialist who worked closely with Rhodes to plot a coup in the South African Republic. The purpose was to enable the British empire to reestablish hegemony over the Transvaal. Rhodes's friend, Leander Starr Jameson, a Scottish doctor, was supposed to guide a mounted column of troops from the British South Africa Company as Uitlanders (non-Afrikaner whites) set up a provisional government in Johannesburg.

The campaign proved a fiasco, with the Uitlanders fighting among themselves and lacking much support, as Rhodes discovered. He attempted to call off the expedition, but Jameson, along with 500 men, swept into the South African Republic in December 1895 and the Uitlanders plotted to take control of Johannesburg. Soon, it became clear that the so-called Jameson Raid had failed, and its leader surrendered on January 2, 1896. Kruger eventually commuted the death sentences meted out to the Uitlander ringleaders, inflicting large monetary fines instead. The South African Republic president also acquired military supplies from Europe, clamped down on the political operations of Uitlanders, and established a closer partnership with the Orange Free Republic. In 1898, Kruger won a sweeping victory in the presidential race.

Only temporarily thwarted, Chamberlain determined that Britain must act more directly to counter growing Afrikaner power in southern Africa. At first, Chamberlain hoped to rely on diplomatic pressure, but he underestimated the competing interests of class, region, and ideology that divided the Afrikaners. He also failed to appreciate the determination of the Boers to maintain their autonomy, along with the self-confidence the 1881 military clash with British soldiers had afforded them.

In 1897, Chamberlain sent ardent imperialist Sir Alfred Milner to serve as high commissioner in South Africa. Milner subscribed to the notion of Anglo-Saxon supremacy, believing that his nation possessed a moral right to hold sway over darker-skinned peoples dwelling on other continents. At the same time, Milner appreciated that the slackening condition of the British empire made it greatly reliant on the South African gold mines. Ignoring those desirous of maintaining the peace, Milner deliberately provoked discontent in the Witwatersrand, resulting in a petition containing more than 21,000 signatures that demanded British intervention and a refusal to allow a peaceful resolution of mining disputes between Kruger's government and Uitlanders.

Notwithstanding painstaking efforts by the Cape colonial government to stave off a conflict, Milner and Chamberlain appeared determined to escalate tensions. Certain that Britain desired to end Transvaal autonomy, the South African Republic and the Orange Free State issued declarations of war in October 1899. Chroniclers have continued to dispute the causes of the conflict, called the South African War, the Anglo-Boer War, or, to Afrikaner nationalists, the Second War of Independence. As Leonard Thompson analyzes, "Britain went to war to reestablish

AFRICANS DURING THE WAR

The South African War helped to determine "which white authority held real power in South Africa," say Rodney Davenport and Christopher Saunders. Those scholars also indicate that the conflict was not allowed "to become a black man's war," although its outbreak engendered early hopes among Africans that their status and influence would soon improve. Indeed, a black elite situated in the Boer republics especially envisioned a British triumph leading to expanded opportunities for blacks, with some even hoping that the war was intended to revise arbitrary borders by transferring land back to Africans. As the fighting began, some blacks moved onto farms vacated by Afrikaners, with the Kgatla Tswana reappropriating land and livestock taken by the Boers.

The ability of Africans in the Transvaal to accomplish more was limited by laws that denied blacks the right to carry arms; nevertheless, Boer fighters relied on blacks to perform a series of chores, including some that were militarily related. The Boers, for their part, complained that the British handed weapons to blacks, who, in turn, "committed horrible atrocities on fugitive or peaceful women and children."* Other South Africans, including the Tswana located in the northern Cape and western Transvaal, the Zulus, and the Pedi, all aided the British in hunting down guerrillas.

Like the Boers, blacks suffered in the camps set up by the British to control the civilian population and ensure the availability of labor. The British deliberately herded African men, women, and children into these camps, compelling the men to work for British soldiers. Expected to attend to their own dietary and housing needs, Africans received barely half the subsistence level of support that whites in the camps did. When the war ended, 29 camps held Africans alone—over 115,000 of them. The death toll steadily mounted, surpassing the 14,000 mark by late 1901.

* Quoted in Davenport and Saunders, *South Africa*, p. 232.

Highlanders capturing Boer guns during the Second Boer War, also called the South African War, about 1900. This Boer War, begun by the British to secure ownership of the diamond mines of the Transvaal and the Orange Free State, degenerated into guerrilla warfare and lasted three years—much longer than expected. The war was a turning point for the British colonial army, and the British Empire in particular, dealing the British a number of setbacks and casualties at great cost.

British hegemony throughout Southern Africa, the republics to preserve their independence."[52] Other historians have pointed to different factors, including economic considerations, piqued by concern about the Witwatersrand gold mines; chauvinistic British attitudes; key figures like Chamberlain and Milner; and competition involving European rivals, particularly Germany. Bill Nasson refers to the Anglo-Boer affair as "the most important colonial war of the early twentieth century."[53]

The actual war, anticipated by the British to be an easy affair, proved taxing and, initially at least, disastrous. This proved so, despite the fact that the British, with some 450,000 soldiers, dwarfed the republics' regiments, which amounted to only 88,000 men in uniform. In addition, the Boers, although they had stockpiled a considerable store of arms, proved unable to add to their weaponry due to the presence of the British Navy and a decision by Portugal to prevent military equipment from passing through Mozambique. Nevertheless, the British experienced a series of defeats at the outset of the conflict, with the sharpest setbacks occurring in Natal. Relying on their experienced commandos, who fervently believed in the fight they were waging, the republics managed to maintain the struggle for two-and-a-half years.

Boer cavalrymen conducted a series of guerrilla strikes against the British, who responded under Lord Horatio Kitchener with a scorched-earth policy regarding farms, crops, and livestock—a tactic long employed against Africans. The British relied on barbed-wire barricades, which connected some 8,000 blockhouses that shielded armed Africans. In addition, Kitchener herded over 100,000 civilians into concentration camps, where sordid conditions allowed epidemic diseases to thrive. Approximately 22,000 British soldiers and 7,000 Boer fighters died in the conflict, which also took the lives of some 28,000 Boer civilians and 20,000 Africans.

The British actions eventually broke the will of the Boer soldiers, with the Treaty of Vereeniging terminating the fighting in May 1902. Commando leader Jan Christian Smuts acknowledged that "humanly speaking" there was "no reasonable chance to retain our independence as Republics." However, Smuts argued, "It clearly becomes our duty to stop the struggle in order that we may perhaps sacrifice our people and our future for a mere idea which cannot be realized."[54] The treaty resulted in the annexation of the Boer republics by Britain, which inflicted no war indemnity on the Boers, promised three million pounds to cover the devastation wreaked, and assured the newly named Orange River Colony and the South African Republic that the question of black suffrage would await self-government. Thus, the South African War led to the redrawing of imperial arbitrary borders yet again, while only cementing the racial boundaries that South African whites had been devising for two-and-a-half centuries.

6

A New
Confederation

Following the South African War, Afrikaners quickly moved to return to power, setting aside the new arbitrary borders that had resulted in the British annexation of the Orange River Colony and the South African Republic. As this process unfolded, tracked by British authorities determined to adopt a conciliatory approach toward the Boers, Africans continued to be afflicted with other kinds of restrictive artificial boundaries. Only eight years passed before the Union of South Africa emerged, a unitary state that joined together the Orange River Colony, the South African Republic, Natal, and the Cape. To the dismay of blacks and liberal whites, the Union of South Africa featured racially exclusionary political practices. Thus, as territorial borders in southern Africa seemingly dissolved, white-black ones only hardened.

Both Transvaal delegates and British representatives argued among themselves as the Vereeniging negotiations took place. High Commissioner Milner hoped to destroy the Boer leadership to pave the way for a fuller British South Africa. Commander in Chief Kitchener, however, reasoned that a policy of conciliation was required to ensure "a reconstructed white settler order."[55] The final peace treaty was more in keeping with Kitchener's perception, enabling the Boers to regroup rather quickly. The period of direct British rule proved to be remarkably brief, ending by 1905. Under British tutelage, Boer farmers, rather than Africans, who made up almost 80 percent of the population, received generous compensation, including land titles and agricultural support. By contrast, the Africans failed to see something they had envisioned: an end to race-based legislation. Indeed, the state actually reinforced controls over laborers in the mining industry, reducing their wages. Eventually, blacks toiled for but one-tenth of the amount that white workers received.

Pressured by mine owners, who were concerned about a severe labor shortage, the colonial government moved to import workers from China. In contrast to Indian laborers in Natal—for whom Mohandas Gandhi had demanded equal treatment, including the right to vote—Chinese workers in the Witwatersrand were compelled to accept a new contract after three years of service or return home. Altogether almost 64,000 Chinese laborers came to South Africa during the 1904–1908

MOHANDAS GANDHI IN SOUTHERN AFRICA

Born in Porbandar, India, on October 2, 1869, Mohandas Gandhi (1869–1948) studied law in England before returning to his native country to practice. In 1893, he went to Natal, where he suffered discriminatory treatment. Within a year, he founded the Natal Indian Congress, and soon became involved in a campaign to oppose legislation that precluded Indians from voting in Natal.

Following the South African War, when he helped to establish an Indian ambulance corps, Gandhi broadened his campaign against discrimination in South Africa, concentrating on the Transvaal. By 1906, he initiated a campaign of nonviolent civil disobedience—rooted in his philosophy of *satyagraha* (soul force)—to oppose the Transvaal registration law requiring Indians to carry passes. Other efforts involved attempts to challenge both the poll tax demanded of Indians and the refusal of South African authorities to recognize Indian marriages. Gandhi became consumed with a determination to end the kinds of arbitrary borders that saddled Indians with discriminatory treatment.

Like other nonwhite and African leaders, Gandhi contested the draft South African constitution, which failed to provide political rights to Indians. He soon also challenged a tax in Natal that fell only on Indian laborers and their families, immigration and travel restrictions that targeted Indians, and encumbrances on their property and trading rights. He helped lead strikes at the coalfields and sugar plantations of Natal, which resulted in his imprisonment and international attention.

Gandhi's efforts partially succeeded: The tax was removed and Indian familial practices, which allowed for polygamous marriages, were no longer restricted. On Gandhi's departure from South Africa in mid-1914, Jan Smuts was heard to declare, "The saint has left our shores, I sincerely hope for ever!"*

Despite Smuts's observation, Gandhi's own political language, as William Beinart points out, clearly distinguished "between 'British Indians,' 'coolies,' and 'Kaffirs' [a racially offensive term for Africans]," and the Indian pacifist made no effort to solicit support from Africans.

* Quoted in Davenport and Saunders, *South Africa*, p. 278.

period, despite opposition from whites, who worried about the impact on jobs and wages. The Chinese resided in compounds, obtained only unskilled positions, and encountered discriminatory treatment, particularly in the areas of commerce and land. The Chinese workers helped to revitalize the mining industry, but the low wages they received crippled African workers, who futilely sought better conditions.

As the economies of the former republics improved, farmers and capitalists benefited. Some attempts were undertaken to assist small farmers. Invariably, those farmers, the vast majority of whom were white, were reduced to sharecropping, where they worked side-by-side with Africans. Impoverished Boers also headed into urban areas, where they encountered British dominance and competed with blacks for jobs.

Despite such mixed economic results and notwithstanding the absence of a system of genuine representation, the Orange River Colony and the Transvaal actually witnessed an expansion of political freedoms. Louis Botha and Jan Smuts created a new political party, Het Volk, in January 1905, while in July, James Barry Munnik Hertzog and Abraham Fischer established Orangie Unie, which proved to be more anti-British. Both organizations demonstrated the potency of Afrikaner nationalism. Each emphasized the importance of ensuring that Dutch or Afrikaans, not English, remained the basic language in the former republics. The Het Volk called for self-government for both the Transvaal and the Orange River Colony.

Increasingly, British leaders viewed South Africa as similar to other settlement colonies within the empire, including Canada, Australia, and New Zealand. Consequently, the British government opted to allow self-government in the Transvaal while hoping to maintain a strong British influence. On February 20, 1907, Transvaal Afrikaners under Botha captured the first general election held under the new constitution, while later in the year, the Orangie Unie, led by Smuts, achieved an even greater electoral triumph. The following February, the South African Party, spearheaded by John X. Merriman and backed by the

Afrikaner Bond, which championed the interests of Afrikaner white farmers, won the Cape Colony election. Natal, which possessed a majority of British voters, remained the lone South African regime supporting British colonial rule.

Botha and Smuts adopted a policy of reconciliation, seeking to smooth over differences between or among Afrikaners and individuals of British ancestry. Speaking at the London Colonial Conference in early 1907, Botha stated, "British interests would be absolutely safe in the hands of the new [Transvaal] cabinet." The Boer political leaders expressed no comparable concerns about indigenous peoples, who continued to suffer from political restrictions and moves to subjugate them. In Natal, whites slaughtered thousands of Africans following the Bambatha Rebellion, the final armed struggle spearheaded by a traditional leader. That uprising erupted after adult African males were compelled to pay a poll tax. The revolt began in mid-1906, led to Bambatha's death, and concluded in northern Natal in 1907.

While approximately two dozen whites perished because of the Bambatha Rebellion, 3,500–4,000 Zulu died, with thousands more jailed and beaten. During the midst of the revolt, Winston Churchill refused to accept the help of German troops, indicating that "in Natal our chief difficulty has not been to kill the rebellious natives, but to prevent our Colonists (*who so thoroughly understand native wars*) from killing too many of them."[56]

Determined to strengthen their hold on political power in places like Natal, where whites were outnumbered by blacks ten to one, the Afrikaners came to support a political confederation of white-dominated colonies in South Africa. Delegates initially gathered in Durban in October 1908, with Smuts offering a constitutional plan already acceptable to leaders of the Transvaal, the Orange River Colony, and the Cape Colony. Natal representatives, favoring a federal state and concerned about white-black relations, appeared more reluctant to support Smuts's proposal. Subsequent meetings in February and May 1909 resulted in a new constitution that established a unitary state within a parliamentary framework. The existing colonies became provinces of the Union of South Africa, while a central government held supreme authority over local institutions. The constitution contained no bill of rights protecting individual liberties, and it established a strong lower house of parliament whose power would not be restrained by a system of checks and balances. With very few exceptions, the document contained few protective measures for South Africa's indigenous peoples.

This was hardly surprising as Smuts, like so many white leaders in the colonies, subscribed to the idea of the white man's burden then in vogue in Europe and the United States. Smuts continued to be guided by a belief in white supremacy, which he had indicated earlier: "The race struggle is destined to assume a magnitude on the African continent such as the world has never seen ... and in that appalling struggle for existence, the unity of the white camp will not be the least necessary condition ... of warding off annihilation." Determined to keep Africans as disfranchised as possible, Smuts explained, "I sympathize profoundly with the native races of South Africa, whose land it was long before we came here.... But I don't believe in politics for them."[57]

Significantly, the four colonies possessed widely divergent franchise laws. The Transvaal and the Orange River Colony allowed only white men to vote or serve in parliament. In Natal, white men with minimal economic qualifications could vote, as could Africans, Indians, and the so-called Coloreds (or mixed races); economic circumstances precluded the vast majority of nonwhites from voting. In the Cape colony, any literate individual with proven financial means could vote or be elected to parliament; in practice, 85 percent of registered voters were white and no black ever became a member of the Cape colonial parliament. The new constitution attempted a compromise regarding suffrage, permitting only white men to serve in parliament and retaining existing franchise measures. In an effort to safeguard the rights of blacks in the Cape colony, delegates agreed that any bill changing existing franchise laws had to receive a two-thirds vote in each house of parliament, meeting jointly.

The constitution contained other important elements,

Jan Christian Smuts (1870–1950). Smuts was born near Riebeeck West in the Cape and attended Cambridge University (England) law school. He entered politics at a young age, becoming State Attorney and advisor to the Executive Council in Paul Kruger's government at 28. He was instrumental in planning the extended guerrilla conflict of the Second Boer War and served as a delegate at the Vereeniging Peace Conference. During World War I, he was a field general and helped to create the Royal Air Force. He followed Botha as Prime Minister. In 1933 Smuts became Deputy Prime Minister and Minister of Justice under Hertzog, taking over as Premier in 1939. He was instrumental in the formation of the United Nations.

including a provision indicating that both English and Dutch would stand as the nation's official languages. The British government was allowed, at an indeterminate date, to further expand the arbitrary borders of the Union of South Africa by incorporating Southern Rhodesia, Basutoland, Bechuanaland Protectorate, and Swaziland. Several delegates called for the immediate incorporation of the other territories in South Africa—something that the British government proved reluctant to support because of opposition from African chiefs.

After the delegates completed their deliberations, many continued to have doubts about the new constitution. The British South Africa Company remained uncertain whether the new government would safeguard its interests. Several white Rhodesians, whose ancestry was largely British, were adverse to residing in a state whose majority was Afrikaner. The Orange River Colony's Native Congress urged the holding of a black Congress, while the South African Native Congress hoped for a meeting of representatives in Bloemfontein.

In March 1909, 38 delegates to the Native Convention passed resolutions condemning the new constitution's racially restrictive clauses and declared itself a permanent body. Black representatives, who were themselves already enfranchised, met in King William's Town the following month, and chose to support the new confederation while urging "concerted action" with the Native Congress.[58]

Notwithstanding such opposition, the various colonial regimes sent delegates to London, while representatives from the various black and nonwhite organizations, along with white sympathizers, traveled abroad seeking support for an eradication of racial barriers. The representatives from those organizations encountered Gandhi, who was also demanding that racial restrictions in South Africa be discarded, and obtained backing from the Anti-Slavery and Aborigines Protection Societies, and from a small number of radical M.P.s (members of Parliament). However, they discovered little support among the British press or in England's Parliament, which voted in 1909 for a measure that again redrew the arbitrary borders that had long characterized southern Africa. The South Africa Act largely replicated the measure agreed to by the South African colonies.

This led to the inauguration of the Union of South Africa, which occurred on May 31, 1910, and resulted in the drawing of new political, racial, and economic arbitrary borders. The establishment of the unitary state, clearly stronger than the separate colonies, appeared to benefit Great Britain. Hopes arose that improved relations would result between the English and Afrikaners, along with the promotion of financial and mining interests. The Liberal government of Britain's prime minister Herbert H. Asquith believed that the interests of Africans would also best be served by a strong union, which contained "4 million Africans, 500,000 Coloureds, 150,000 Indians, and 1,275,000 Whites."[59] As Robert Ross indicates, the British "hoped, vainly, that the liberal traditions of the Cape would in time be spread to the rest of the country."[60]

The defeat of the Boer republics during the South African War failed to dampen the determination of Afrikaners to establish their own kinds of arbitrary borders, whether territorial, political, or racial. For their part, the British were inclined to adopt a conciliatory approach while generally accepting the Boers' attempts to create a racially regimented society that most benefited Afrikaners and others of European extract. This only encouraged whites who were residing in the Orange River Colony and the Transvaal to set up forceful Afrikaner nationalist organizations, which in turn agitated for self-government.

These concerns about the demographic realities in southern Africa, heightened by the Bambatha Rebellion and other indications of unhappiness among the nonwhite populations, encouraged movement toward a confederation of the region's white-controlled colonies. That culminated in the eventual establishment of the Union of South Africa, which would serve as a model—in form, if not in substance—of a unitary state determined to maintain rigid arbitrary barriers of race and class.

7

The Union
of South Africa

Following its founding in 1910, the Union of South Africa soon became dominated by Afrikaners, who sought to create a segregationist state separated from the British Commonwealth. As color barriers lengthened, black opposition arose, resulting in the formation of South African Native National Congress (SANNC), which came to be known as the African National Congress (ANC). Thus, Afrikaners sought to discard the imperial ties (or arbitrary border) that tied them to Great Britain, while creating rigidly constructed artificial boundaries of a racial cast. Black opponents, in turn, fought against racial discrimination, soon splintering into moderate and more militant factions. All of this occurred in the midst of a marked increase in the national income, notwithstanding the onset of the Great Depression and movement toward virtual economic self-sufficiency at the close of World War II.

From its onset, the South African government sought to strengthen "white power in the new state," Leonard Thompson reports.[61] The first general election, held in September 1910, produced a victory for Louis Botha and Jan Smuts, with Botha serving as prime minister. For the time being, they accepted the new nation's participation in the British empire while seeking greater autonomy for the white settler-controlled dominions. However, Botha and Smuts, who favored reconciliation between Afrikaners and English-speaking whites, became increasingly dependent on support from South Africans with British origins. That alienated Afrikaners, with the Orange Free State leader Barry Munnik Hertzog establishing the National Party in 1914, which was popular with less affluent Afrikaner rural voters, intellectuals, and various businessmen and professionals.

Africans too proved unhappy, forming the South African Native National Congress (1912), led by Pixley ka Isaka Seme, Alfred Mangena, Richard Msimang, and George Montsiosa, all "mission-educated Christians who had qualified as lawyers in England."[62] The organization battled against legal discrimination, including that contained in the Natives Land Act (1913). That measure attempted to regularize land policy by imposing territorial segregation. Africans, who made up over 70 percent of the population, could only purchase or acquire title to land within the reserves, which amounted to but 7 percent of South African territory. The Natives Land Act did anticipate the reserves' acquiring more land, particularly in the Transvaal and

THE "COLOUREDS"

During the opening stages of the nineteenth century, white inhabitants of the Cape colony continued to view themselves as distinct from people of color, including Khoikhoi, blacks and those of mixed descent. The termination of slavery in 1838 resulted in new arbitrary borders based on race, with white workers particularly determined to keep themselves apart from Africans. The large influx of blacks in the western Cape region by the close of the century led to a heightened desire by the so-called Coloured—or mixed-race nonwhite—people, who possessed some European origin, to be viewed distinctively.

Initially, this group included the Khoisan and former slaves. Like the Boers, they spoke Afrikaans, not English, but occupied only an intermediate stage within South Africa's racial framework, which the government categorized into four broad racial groups: whites, Bantu-speaking Africans, Asians, and "Coloureds." The pass laws did not apply to this last group, which also suffered no restrictions on entering urban centers. Still, they endured segregationist laws, discriminatory treatment, and franchise restrictions. Economic discrimination heightened during Hertzog's tenure as prime minister. Even harsher restrictions occurred following World War II, when the system of apartheid emerged.

Paralleling "the ambivalent position of Coloureds" inside South African society and the nature of the arbitrary borders affecting them, their political involvement proved halting at best.* For 35 years, the physician and politician Abdullah Abdurahman guided the largely middle-class African Political Organization (or African People's Organization) down a moderate path, supporting assimilation and a conciliatory approach. During the Depression era and World War II, more radical forces emerged, including the National Liberation League and the Anti-Coloured Affairs Department, which joined the Non-European Unity Movement.

* Quoted in Christopher Saunders and Nicholas Southey, *Historical Dictionary of South Africa*, 2nd edition. Lanham, Maryland: Scarecrow Press, 2000, p. 66.

the Orange Free State. A commission, headed by Sir William Beaumont, began exploring the issue of how much land the reserves should hold.

The outbreak of World War I produced a political crisis in South Africa, with many Afrikaners, including a number of German descent, recalling the support they had received from Germany during the South African conflict. Most Afrikaners appeared desirous of remaining neutral as fighting erupted in Europe, but Botha and Smuts fervently supported the British war effort, heeding the cabinet's demand that South African forces invade German South West Africa. The Nationalists opposed the proposal, while the Transvaal and Free State commandants also contested it. Botha and Smuts—later celebrated for his wartime adventures, including forays into German East Africa and service in the British Imperial War Cabinet—led South African troops into the neighboring protectorate, which induced some Afrikaners to participate in an armed rebellion.

The Afrikaner rebel Colonel Manie Maritz departed, along with his followers, for German South West Africa as a plot to terminate the union unfolded. The government quickly quelled the rebellion, but the execution of one young officer, Captain Jopie Fourie, enraged many Afrikaners. The 1915 elections saw Nationalists garner nearly as many votes as Botha's South African National Party. Economic conditions influenced the results, with many small farmers upset by the impoverishment that afflicted them and because of the purported sense of cultural superiority displayed by wealthy farmers who spoke English.

Still more upsetting to poor Afrikaners was the comfortable economic situation of certain well-educated blacks and Indians, who also appeared to enjoy English culture. Consequently, calls intensified for action to cement white supremacy. Simultaneously, white miners conducted strikes in 1913 and 1914, with the latter labor upheaval leading to the declaration of martial law and the employment of a new defense force. Strikes by black laborers resulted in even harsher treatment, including the murder of scores of strikers. These disturbances heightened the popularity of Frederic Creswell's South African Labour Party, which sought better conditions for white workers and directly advocated racial segregation. The Labour Party was divided about the war, with a pacifist section establishing the International Socialist League.

Hardly pleasing to Afrikaners was the fact that some 34,000 blacks volunteered to assist with the drive into South West Africa, although they were allowed to serve only as noncombatants. Over 20,000 members of the South African Native Labour Contingent traveled overseas, confronting hostile treatment from officials, along with segregation. This occurred despite King George V's speech to the unit, in which he declared, "You also are part of my great armies fighting for the liberty and freedom of all my subjects of all races and creeds throughout the Empire."[63]

In fact, segregation practices remained in place in South Africa, notwithstanding the acknowledgment by the Beaumont Commission in 1916 that the present reserves were inadequate, requiring millions of additional acres of arable land to become viable. The legislature passed a Native Administration Bill (1917), which sought to keep native and European administration apart; this displeased liberals in the former Cape colony and black leaders.

In late 1915, Botha had sent a unit of 6,000 soldiers to Britain; that contingent soon helped defend the Suez Canal from an Turkish onslaught, participated in the bloody battle of the Somme, held Delville Wood just east of the village of Longueval, moved into Belgium, and suffered many casualties before surrendering to the Germans near the end of the war. In the meantime, Smuts attempted a takeover of German East Africa but was temporarily thwarted by the German commander Von Lettow-Vorbeck. These aggressive moves further infuriated many Nationalists, who viewed Botha and Smuts as traitors to South African whites. Nevertheless, the two men represented their state at the Versailles Conference following the end of World War I, warning that harsh treatment of the Germans would result in a new conflagration or anarchy. Smuts did prove instrumental in the establishment of the League of Nations, which anticipated reliance on collective security to be necessary.

The reworking of colonial Africa proved less happy for Smuts and Botha, who had hoped that South Africa would acquire the protectorates of Southern Rhodesia and German South West Africa. Having finally occupied German East Africa, Smuts believed he might be able to trade it to Portugal for Mozambique, which would have further broadened South Africa's already expanded arbitrary borders. All of this suggested the artificial quality of imperial control and territorial possessions. Neither the Rhodesians nor the Portuguese were interested in Smuts's plan, while the British worried about South Africa's treatment of blacks. Thus, South Africa held sway over South West Africa, but only through a League of Nations mandate that was limited. Botha and Smuts also unsuccessfully sought control of the British High Commission territories of Basutoland, Bechuanaland, and Swaziland.

Shortly following Botha's death in 1919, Smuts suffered another setback when the Nationalist and the Labour parties received more votes than the Unionists in general elections. South Africa also experienced more strikes and protests against both the pass laws and conditions in the mine fields, leading to the killing of scores of blacks. The SANNC continued to demand an end to the pass system, adopting the Gandhian tactic of nonviolent protest, but violence still occurred.

In late 1921, white laborers became enraged on learning that employers intended to discard barriers pertaining to nonwhite semiskilled labor. White workers went on strike, supported by both the Nationalist and the Labour parties. Afrikaners turned themselves into armed commandos, resulting in the declaration of martial law. Fierce fighting led to over 200 deaths, with Smuts receiving much of the blame for the bloodletting. The Nationalists and the Labour Party agreed to a compact, while Hertzog reached out to Coloured people,

James Barry Munnik Hertzog (1866–1942), a South African military and political leader. He served as a judge in the Orange Free State and commanded a division of Boer forces in the Second Boer War. Hertzog opposed Louis Botha and British rule, which took him out of the running for political office and pushed him to found the National Party. He eventually served as prime minister for 15 years, until September 1939, passing legislation favoring racial segregation and advocating neutrality in World War II.

urging that the economic color bar affecting them be lifted and calling for their receipt of the franchise in northern provinces. In April 1924, Smuts left his post as prime minister.

Hertzog took over as head of the South African government, with the Nationalists and the Labour Party capturing the 1924 general elections. During Hertzog's initial nine-year reign as prime minister of the Union of South Africa, his administration passed social welfare legislation that protected white urban tenants, miners, other workers, and white farmers. White women received the right to vote, shrinking the percentage of black voters in the Cape province. A drive for bilingualism in the civil service led to Afrikaans being considered an official state language. A Colour Bar Act sought to shield skilled and semiskilled white laborers, in keeping with the new prime minister's belief that separate provisions were necessary to protect the white community:

> The Europeans must keep to a standard of living which shall meet the demands of white civilization. Civilization and standards of living always go hand in hand. Thus a white cannot exist on a native wage scale, because this means that he has to give up his own standard of living and [take] on the standard of living of the native. In short, the white man becomes a white kaffir (an African).[64]

Hertzog also pushed hard for greater autonomy for South Africa. At the Imperial Conference held in London in late 1926, Hertzog revealed that he already considered South Africa to be, in effect, "completely independent ... just as free as England itself." He deemed the only formal legal connection to involve the "personal bond of a common king," while warning that separatist movements would likely emerge if no clear declaration of equal status occurred. At the conference, British prime minister Stanley Baldwin and the heads of the dominions crafted the Balfour Declaration. That document presented those territorial entities as "autonomous communities within the British Empire, in no way subordinate to another in any aspect of their domestic or external affairs, though united by a common allegiance to the Crown and freely associated as members of the British Commonwealth of Nations."[65]

The South African government established a Department of External Affairs, which led to the placement of diplomats in major international centers, including the headquarters of the League of Nations in Geneva, and the appointments of trade commissioners in Europe and North America. Hertzog continued his predecessors' efforts to acquire control of Swaziland, Bechuanaland, and Basutoland, again to no avail, blundering in the issuance of threats to engage in economic protectionism.

Serving as his own native affairs minister, Hertzog remained determined to solidify segregationist policies, declaring early in his administration that "territorial segregation of the natives is the only sound policy that can be followed both for the natives and the Europeans in South Africa." Africans, Hertzog insisted, needed to make the reserves economically productive. However, whites would receive preferential treatment in general, with Hertzog somewhat defensively acknowledging, "The native cannot blame us if in the first place we try to find work for our own class." Thus, he supported an industrial color bar intended to benefit white laborers.

In a move designed to somewhat placate Africans, Hertzog, in November 1925, called for additional lands to be added to the reserves. All the while, he held back legislation designed to afford suffrage to indigenous peoples, and actually supported a measure reducing the amount of acreage proposed for the reserves. The Immorality Act of 1927 criminalized nonmarital sexual relations between whites and blacks. The Native Administration Act of 1929 established labor districts throughout South Africa, placing all black workers "under the discipline of pass laws and movement control." Other legislation erected "a system of arbitrary labour controls," which fell on workers and their families alike.[66]

The onslaught of repressive legislation led black forces to unite, at least to some extent, in no longer acquiescing to the system of segregation. Portions of the African National Congress (formerly the SANCC) adopted a more militant stance, urging that passes be contested. Blacks proved unconvinced that promises of additional lands in the reserves would make up for the loss of political rights. Certain ANC members shifted leftward, influenced by the black nationalist perspective of Marcus Garvey, a Jamaican immigrant living in the United States who directed the Back-to-Africa campaign. Some became attracted to communism, in contrast to Clements Kadalie, the head of the Industrial and Commercial Workers' Union of South Africa (ICU), whose emphasis on land policies, wages, and pass laws particularly appealed to rural blacks. For a time, the ICU became a mass movement, but soon foundered, because of heavy-handed government practices.

Divisions in government ranks led to a general election campaign in 1929, during which Thielman Roos and Daniel F. Malan raised fears of racial miscegenation. They portrayed Smuts, a committed white supremacist, as favoring a "Kaffir state ... a black hegemony in which we are all to be on an equal footing." The Nationalists ended up with an electoral majority, strengthening the hand of extremist elements. The new minister of justice, Oswald Pirow, called on the newly passed Riotous Assembly Act to employ "strong arm-tactics," particularly against blacks.[67] Schisms prevented the ANC and the ICU from responding adequately to the latest repressive actions.

The advent of the Great Depression, which became a worldwide phenomenon by the beginning of the 1930s, compelled the South African regime to concentrate on other concerns, including its very economic viability. The severity of the economic situation led to a new coalition government in 1933, with Hertzog remaining prime minister and Smuts serving as deputy prime minister. The following December, a fusion of the National and Unionist parties led to the formation of the United South African Nationalist Party (the United Party). In addition to improving South Africa's economic situation, the founders of the United Party hoped to determine the nation's status within the British Empire.

For his part, Hertzog believed that a South Africa-first strategy, along with full equality regarding the English and Afrikaans languages, would allow for white unity. Indeed, the South African government now passed the Native Representation Act

(1936) that dramatically restricted the political rights of Africans in the Cape province and generally strengthened racial segregation. Such measures failed to satisfy more rabid segregationists like Malan, who established the Purified National Party, while some of Smuts's English-speaking followers from Natal founded the Dominion Party under Colonel C.F. Stallard. Many Afrikaner nationalists again demonstrated their disdain for the British Empire, while poor, urban Afrikaners joined cultural organizations like the Ossewa Brandwag (OB), which was founded shortly after a centenary celebration of the Great Trek. Afrikaner groups like the OB, the Purified National Party, and the Afrikaner Broederbond came to feature "a simple racist, totalitarian mode based on the German ... fascist model."[68]

As Leonard Thompson indicates, the difficulty of obtaining arms, coupled with cultural and historical differences, inhibited the resistance of Africans to the system of segregation they confronted. Thompson writes, "Indian and Coloured South Africans had little in common with one another or with Africans, and were themselves disunited."[69] Most Indians, who made up 2 percent of the population and resided in Natal and the southern Transvaal, were Hindus, and failed to identify with the other nonwhites in South Africa. Nonwhites, a group four times larger than the Indian group, generally dwelled in the Cape province and were themselves ethnically, culturally, and economically splintered. An elite group of nonwhite people, both Muslim and Christian, faced a diminution of their status, including newly devised legal discrimination, while the much greater number of poor nonwhite Cape residents also suffered because of social disfunctionality, including criminality and alcoholism. Interestingly, many nonwhites held similar attitudes about Africans as did whites. Africans, who still comprised approximately 70 percent of the South African population by the mid-1930s, possessed distinct historical backgrounds and interests of their own.

Domestic issues were hardly the only ones to influence South African politics during this period. Charles Te Water, the

London high commissioner throughout the decade, condemned the Japanese incursion into Manchuria in 1931, while the South African regime, led by Hertzog and Smuts, supported economic sanctions against Fascist Italy after its attack on Haile Selasse's Ethiopia in 1935. Other top government officials supported the continuance of subsidies for Italian shippers who skirted around the Cape and the delivery of farm products to Mussolini's soldiers in northern Africa. By contrast, Te Water, who became president of the League of Nations' General Assembly in 1933, called for an oil embargo against Italy. The eventual Italian triumph in Ethiopia, coupled with the outbreak of the Spanish Civil War and the invasion of China by Japan, dampened hopes of various South African politicians regarding the League's effectiveness.

While both Hertzog and Smuts originally indicated that South Africa should adopt a neutralist stance if Great Britain went to war against another European state, the German takeover of the Sudetenland in Czechoslovakia convinced Smuts that Germany had to be stopped. In September 1939, as war erupted in Europe, the South African parliament convened, with Hertzog insisting on a position of neutrality. Smuts prevailed, however, convincing a majority in parliament to break off diplomatic relations with Germany. The cabinet remained divided, as the Labour and the Dominion parties backed Smuts and Malan's Nationalists supported Hertzog.

The prime minister subsequently resigned, joined by 37 Afrikaner parliamentarians from the United Party. Smuts, who was backed by all the English-speaking South Africans and many Afrikaners, took over the reigns of government and immediately issued a declaration of war against Germany. Hertzog, along with many of his followers, linked up with Malan to form the Reunited National, or People's, Party. The two men soon broke, however, for Hertzog had come to view English speakers as authentic South Africans.

Led by J.F.J. van Rensburg, the OB created paramilitary forces, the Stormjaers, that employed uniforms obviously patterned after those sported by Fascists. Louis Weichardt's pro-Fascist Greyshirts espoused anti-Semitism. To prevent revolutionary action, Prime Minister Smuts demanded that rifles be surrendered to public authorities. Indeed, by 1942, members of the OB proceeded to carry out acts of sabotage intended to disrupt the war effort. By contrast, Malan remained committed to electoral processes, and prevented the OB from dominating Afrikaner nationalist ranks. Still, many Afrikaners continued to await a German victory in World War II, believing that would allow for the establishment of an Afrikaner republic.

Nevertheless, nearly 400,000 individuals made up South Africa's military forces during the conflagration, with some 123,000 blacks performing noncombatant roles. Smuts guided his nation into the conflict, believing that "this glorious mother continent of Western civilization—the proudest achievement of the human spirit up to date," was imperiled.[70] South African soldiers participated in the liberation of Ethiopia, swept into Madagscar to prevent a takeover by the Japanese, joined in campaigns in northern Africa, Egypt, and Libya, and battled on Italian soil and in the skies over Poland. South Africa provided valuable minerals to the Allies during the war, including gold, platinum, and uranium.

On the domestic front, the Smuts-led government enacted social welfare reforms, including compensation for industrial accidents, pensions, unemployment coverage, health care, and secondary education. By the last half of 1942, the government had adopted a more lax attitude on pass laws and established commissions that examined the nation's racial difficulties. Government reports condemned the reserve system and the exploitation of migrant labor while calling for more welfare benefits, albeit within a segregated framework. The employment color bar slackened during the war, wages of black factory workers rose, Africans became eligible for various old-age and disability pensions, and African education received greater government support.

All the while, Smuts continued to view Africans paternalistically while affirming that "everybody in this country is agreed

Jan Smuts's determination that Hitler be stopped prevailed over Hertzog's position of neutrality during World War II, and the South African Air Force joined
Allied Forces to drive Germany's General Rommel from North Africa. South
African soldiers aided in the liberation of Ethiopia, the prevention of a Japanese
takeover of Madagascar, campaigns in Egypt and Libya, and air and land battles
in Italy and Poland.

that European and African should live apart and preserve their
respective cultures."[71] A new crop of black leaders saw matters
differently, however, with the ANC, by 1943, emphasizing the
need for discarding racially restrictive legislation, for the redistribution of land, for the right of Africans to bargain collectively,
and for universal adult suffrage. Africans in Johannesburg, beset
by soaring transportation costs, carried out at least a pair of bus
boycotts, while squatter movements challenged the housing
shortage they confronted. A new Youth League, which included
Nelson Rohihlahla Mandela as a founding member, emerged
within the ANC.

From the time of its establishment in 1910 through the end of
World War II, the Union of South Africa confronted internal
divisions regarding both domestic policies and its status within
the British empire. Afrikaners, particularly Louis Botha, Jan
Smuts, Barry Munnik Hertzog, and Daniel F. Malan, dominated
national politics, with all agreeing on the need for racial segregation. However, they disagreed on how to construct arbitrary

borders of a racial cast and on how restrictive those barriers should be to sustain a segregationist state. The Afrikaner leaders also grappled with another issue involving artificial boundaries: the place the Union should occupy within the British Commonwealth. Other groups wrestled for their own place in the South African sun, including Africans, Indians, and other nonwhites, with all chafing at the racial restrictions and territorial restraints that confronted them.

8

South Africa's System of Apartheid

Shortly following the end of World War II, South Africa began to institute a system of apartheid, which was rooted in long-standing historical, cultural, economic, and racial barriers. The National Party championed this policy of separation, moving to strengthen and broaden the segregation that already character-ized South African society. This occurred as African nationalism surged forth across the continent, troubling white supremacists who became still more determined to maintain racial divides, including those of a territorial variety. Thus, South Africa con-tinued to experience the conundrum the region had endured from the beginning of Dutch and English colonialism: how white political and cultural control could prevail in the face of a hostile nonwhite African majority.

Following World War II, Afrikaners, almost without excep-tion, hoped that the South African government would act to solidify white supremacy. Farmers and commercial operators foresaw unrestricted access to African labor, whose distribution and discipline, they believed, should be carefully controlled by the government. However, Afrikaner laborers desired no compe-tition from black workers. Certain intellectuals, including soci-ology professor G.S. Cronje, called for South Africa's economic and political spheres to be fully segregated. The Sauer Report, devised for the National Party, urged that a system of apartheid be implemented and declared Indians to be incapable of assim-ilation, Africans to be appropriate subjects for a Native Industrial Development Corporation, the reserves to be in need of consolidation, and "Coloureds" to be racially distinct enough to require separation from whites, possibly even to the extent of having specific lands set aside for them. The report also demanded that representation be denied blacks and that mis-sionary societies be excluded from the field of black education.

In March 1946, the South African government passed the Asiatic Land Tenure and Indian Representation Bill, which restricted Indian ownership while allowing Indians to be repre-sented by whites in parliament. The Natal Indian Congress (NIC) conducted a passive resistance campaign in response, resulting in 2,000 arrests. By August, more than 70,000 African miners were on strike, demanding increased wages and an end to restrictions on union organizing. The government responded with considerable violence, then quickly moved to try top communist figures, including W.H. Andrews and Moses Kotane. In March 1947, the NIC agreed to a "Joint Declaration of Co-Operation" with the Transvaal Indian Congress and the ANC calling for full voting rights, equality in the workplace, the discarding of land restrictions, free compulsory education, an end to the pass system, a halt to restrictions on travel by Indians between provinces, and the termination of discriminatory legislation. The Natives Representative Council, proposed by

THE AFRICAN NATIONAL CONGRESS

In January 1912, tribal chiefs and religious leaders, including J.W. Dube, a Zule Methodist minister, helped to found the South African Native National Congress in Bloemfontein, in an effort to champion the rights of black Africans. The Native National Congress determinedly contested the arbitrary borders of both a racial and territorial nature that relegated Africans to an inferior status in South Africa. Within two years, Reverend Dube spearheaded a delegation that traveled to England to condemn the Native Land Act (1913), which set aside a mere 8 percent of South Africa's territory for black occupants.

The Native National Congress undertook a campaign in 1919 against the pass laws in the Transvaal region. In 1923, the organization became the African National Congress and proved to be influenced by the Indian pacifist Mohandas Gandhi. By 1926, the ANC joined with leaders from the Indian community to support integration and democracy in southern Africa.

The ANC engaged in nonviolent resistance against apartheid practices while acquiring greater support among urban blacks and liberal whites. However, in 1944, the ANC Youth League appeared and subsequently pushed for more militant action, which included the Defiance Campaign during the 1950s, which urged that apartheid legislation be violated. The South African regime responded by arresting and banning campaign leaders, in addition to passing still harsher laws.

Hertzog back in 1935, insisted on "a policy which recognizes that Africans are citizens of this country and not things apart."[72]

As opposition by nonwhite peoples continued, even in the face of newly drawn restrictive legislation and outright repression, the general election of May 26, 1948, took place. The recent immigration of 60,000 Europeans influenced the election results, with many Afrikaners believing that the government sought to "plough the Afrikaner under."[73] Notwithstanding an alliance between the Unionists and the Labour Party, the Nationalists triumphed, setting the stage for the construction of an apartheid state. Daniel Malan, having promised to sustain white supremacy in South Africa, replaced Jan Smuts as prime

Increasingly, the ANC found like-minded allies in the South African Indian Congress, the South African Coloured People's Organization, the largely white Congress of Democrats, and the South African Congress of Trade Unions. In 1956, these groups participated in the Congress of the People, which drew up the Freedom Charter, demonstrating support for social democracy and racial equality. Soon, however, divisions arose within the ranks of the ANC, leading to the formation of the Pan African Congress (PAC). PAC militants increasingly attacked the ANC for its supposedly timid approach.

Resorting to armed resistance following the Sharpeville Massacre in early 1960, the ANC, like the PAC, was declared illegal by the South African government. Insisting that apartheid must be terminated and all South Africans enfranchised, the ANC established a liberation army, Umkhonto Wesizwe, and called for economic sabotage. In 1962, the government charged ANC vice president Nelson Mandela and other top black activists with sabotage. Their convictions resulted in lengthy incarcerations, with Mandela jailed for nearly three decades.

The ANC adopted a two-pronged approach, involving both a campaign of direct action inside South Africa and efforts to obtain diplomatic support abroad. Following his election in 1989, President F.W. de Klerk lifted the legal sanctions on the ANC and subsequently released Mandela from prison.

minister. While swearing allegiance to Britain's King George VI, Malan declared South Africa would allow no "external" interference by Great Britain "in our domestic affairs."[74]

Malan moved to more fully incorporate South West Africa within the Union of South Africa, enabling it to be represented in parliament. The action resulted in criticism from the United Nations General Assembly. He also urged the takeover of Basutoland, Bechuanaland, and Swaziland, while insisting that South Africa had no intention of withdrawing, from the British Commonwealth so long as none of her rights were abridged, including the right to establish a republic.

The newly elected parliament proceeded to establish arbitrary borders based on ethnicity and citizenship. The South African Citizenship Bill of 1949 markedly lessened the possibility that a new influx of British immigrants would diminish the Afrikaner majority. Indeed, the government now discarded the previous administration's plan to encourage immigration from Great Britain, favoring instead immigrants from the European continent. The new measure also curtailed opportunities for immigrants to become South African citizens, to the dismay of English-speakers. That discomfiture was heightened by the emergence within the National Party of a separatist faction, led by Johannes G. Strijdom, that urged South Africa to become a republic and withdraw from the British Commonwealth.

In October 1951, a spokesman for the National Party asserted "that South Africa is a sovereign independent State, possessing all the rights to carry out all State functions in the fullest international sense." He affirmed that the party believed "a Republican form of Government, separated from the British Crown, is most suited to the traditions, circumstances and aspirations of the South African people." The National Party also subscribed to the notion that nonwhites made up "a permanent part of the population under the Christian guardianship of the European races" but strongly opposed the transcending of racial boundaries.[75]

Members of the National Party were more in agreement

about actions undertaken to prevent racial integration. The newly constituted government moved quickly, banning military training for nonwhites and eventually proceeding with a plan to disenfranchise the Cape colony's mixed nonwhite citizens. The Prohibition of Mixed Marriages Act and the Immorality Act worked to prevent mixed marriages, including those formed outside South Africa, and to criminalize interracial sex. The Population Registration Act classified individuals according to race, even if that led to the breakup of families; the measure also compelled individuals to carry identity cards indicating their race. The Group Areas Act enforced residential segregation, often compelling mixed nonwhites and Indians to relocate, even when that required the demolition of existing buildings. The Reservation of Separate Amenities Act mandated segregation at beaches, on buses, and in hospitals, schools, and parks.

Befitting the Cold War era in which it was devised, the Suppression of Communism Act targeted the Communist Party, whose leaders disbanded the organization but soon headed underground. The Illegal Squatters Act allowed unwanted indigenous peoples to be removed from urban areas (and, in fact, from any other locations), while the Abolition of Passes Act compelled Africans over the age of 16 to carry passes wherever they traveled. The Tomlinson Commission, operating under the assumption that South Africa could never experience racial equality (as its eventual report would indicate), urged that the reserves be readied to hold the vast bulk of Africans, with local self-government to be allowed in Bantusans. The reserves evolved into a series of territories, with each becoming "a 'homeland' for a potential African 'nation.'"[76]

The government's efforts to disenfranchise nonwhite voters resulted in former servicemen, led by Louis Kane-Berman and Adolf Gysbert "Sailor" Malan, a top-flight pilot who had participated in the Battle of Britain, waging protests, including torchlight processions, against the national government. They formed the War Veterans' Action Committee, or Torch Commando, but soon welcomed nonveterans too, acquiring approximately

120,000 members in some 350 branches. Afrikaners linked up with English-speaking whites, who nevertheless made up the vast bulk of the Torch Commando's membership.

While opposing apartheid, the Torch Commando refused to allow mixed nonwhites to join their ranks but still envisioned a time when nonwhites could assist in wresting political power away from the National Party. Nevertheless, the Torch Commando, which lacked a real program, foundered, eventually opting to form an alliance with the United Party and the Labour Party.

The ANC also continued to oppose the efforts by Daniel Malan's government to establish a state based on apartheid. Shortly following the establishment of that regime, the ANC initiated a "Programme of Action" that urged the use of boycotts, strikes, and civil disobedience. In December 1951, the ANC asked Malan to support an end to legislation sustaining segregation and to back direct participation by blacks in parliament. The following April, the ANC and the South African Indian Congress called for a "defiance campaign" of civil disobedience to challenge pass laws, residential segregation, voter disfranchisement, and anticommunist measures, among other actions. The effort, orchestrated by James Moroka and Yusuf Dadoo, continued until November 1952, producing over 8,300 arrests and a backlash that led to the passage of revised Public Safety and Criminal Law Amendment acts. The government acquired the power to declare a state of emergency, which included the ability to suspend parliamentary measures. The Criminal Law Amendment Bill made it illegal to engage in passive resistance against statutory enactments and authorized fines, imprisonment, and whippings of offenders. The campaign did, however, enable ANC to achieve greater notoriety, with its membership increasing four-fold to 100,000. A young attorney, Nelson Mandela, guided volunteer demonstrators during the protests.

Nevertheless, in April 1953, the National Party improved on its showing in the previous general election, seemingly strengthening the hand of segregationists. The following month, the

South African Party, led by Margaret Ballinger and the author Alan Paton, emerged, welcoming all comers and promising to fight for equal rights. The pro-British Union Federal Party also appeared, headed by individuals such as G. Heaton Nicolls, who had been involved with the Torch Commando.

The new party promised to seek opportunities for all residents of South Africa, even while the Malan government continued its drive to cement apartheid through arbitrary legalistic borders—including the Native Labour Act, designed to control black labor by preventing blacks from participating in work stoppages. The Reservation of Separate Amenities Act expanded segregation to travel and public places, while seemingly deferring to a recent supreme court ruling mandating separate but equal facilities for whites and nonwhites.

In October 1953, both the Anglican Church and the Methodist Church condemned apartheid, deeming it immoral, thereby demonstrating that Malan's attempt to solidify legal segregation would not go unchallenged by major institutional forces in South Africa. Nevertheless, by year's end, Prime Minister Malan insisted that the intermingling by white and nonwhites must come to an end at the universities of Cape Town and Witwatersrand, where English speakers studied.

In January 1954, a new right-wing organization appeared, the Independent United Party, soon (in November) renamed the Conservative Party. The next month, the parliament passed the Riotous Assemblies and Suppression of Communism Amendment Act, soon followed by the Natives Resettlement Act, which allowed for blacks to be forcibly removed from western Johannesburg to Meadowlands. In April, Malan called for the British protectorates of Basutoland, Bechuanaland, and Swaziland to be handed over to South Africa, but British prime minister Winston Churchill indicated that such a transfer would only occur if the inhabitants of those territories agreed, along with the British parliament.

Perhaps to make up for that failure, the National Party soon declared South West Africa to be part of South Africa, challenging

UN stewardship. Led by Nationalists, the Cape provincial council voted in August to extend apartheid throughout the province. The Conservative Party appeared in November 1954, championing apartheid and planning to represent Afrikaners only. Late that month, the 80-year-old Malan resigned, replaced by Johannes G. Strydom from the Transvaal, who fervently supported apartheid.

By February 1955, the government began forcibly resettling blacks in segregated townships in the Cape Western province. Parliament passed the Departure from the Union Regulation Bill, tightening passport provisions, as the government acknowledged it could prevent its opponents from traveling. Relations with India, already contentious, continued to deteriorate, owing to concerns by Indian prime minister Jawaharlal Nehru about South Africa's racial policies.

Once again, the ANC responded to the swirl of events in South Africa by condemning the government's support for apartheid. In late June 1955, 3,000 delegates participated in the Congress of the People, which gathered in Kliptown, just outside Johannesburg, after invitations were delivered by the ANC, the South African Indian Congress, the South African Coloured People's Congress, the newly formed South African Congress of Trade Unions, and other organizations. The Congress of the People issued a Freedom Charter, patterned after the UN Universal Declaration of Human Rights. The charter declared that "South Africa belongs to all who live in it, black and white, and that no government can justly claim authority unless it is based on the will of the people."[77] The document demanded equality under the law, along with basic human rights, including those involving political freedoms, unrestricted movement, religion, the workplace, medical care, and education. The Freedom Charter also called for public control of natural resources, banks, and noncompetitive businesses as well as redistribution of land.

Such proposals failed to dampen the government's enthusiasm for apartheid. In April 1956, Cape Town's public transit became segregated, leading to a call for a bus boycott, supported by the ANC, the South African Coloured People's Organization, and the white South African Congress of Democrats. Refusing to back down, the government passed the Industrial Coalition Act, allowing various skilled labor jobs to be performed by whites only, and the Native (Urban Areas) Amendment Act, empowering local governments to summarily expel blacks deemed threats to law and order.

Late in the year, prosecutors charged scores of top apartheid foes, including ANC leaders Albert J. Luthuli, Oliver Tambo, and Walter Sisulu, with treason and the intent to establish a communist-style government. Violent protests ensued, leading to the deployment of hundreds of policemen. By year's end, a lack of evidence resulted in the dismissal of charges against many defendants, including Luthuli, who supported a nonviolent path to reform and subsequently received the Nobel Peace Prize. In January 1958, the trial proceeded against 95 activists but remained unresolved for over three years, at which point all the remaining defendants were freed. In the meantime, the government moved to enforce segregation in libraries, entertainment venues, schools, and churches.

Notwithstanding the mass conspiracy trial and additional repressive action by the government, the ANC and other progressive organizations, both black and multiracial, continued to condemn South Africa's segregation system. The Federation of South African Women, led by Lilian Ngoyi and Helen Joseph, among others, led a march of 20,000 women on August 9, 1956, in Pretoria, condemning the extension of pass laws to women. The following January, black leaders spearheaded a bus boycott, following an increase in fares in the region between Johannesburg and Pretoria. Some blacks became discontented with the ANC, which was aligned with white allies, demanding a wholly African movement. Guided by Robert Sobukwe, Africanists, in 1959, formed the Pan-Africanist Congress (PAC), which championed social democracy and called for Africa for the Africans.

As late as 1982, when this photograph was taken, racial segregation reigned in South Africa. The black woman framed in the bus window, just below the sign designating the bus for "Non-whites only," tells the tale. Although slavery was abolished in South Africa in 1838, apartheid, or the segregation of non-whites from whites, was only lifted in 1994 after years of bloodshed.

Also, in January 1957, the recently elected South African prime minister, Hendrik F. Verwoerd, an ardent champion of apartheid, called for the establishment of Bantustans—separate and supposedly autonomous black African states. A partial response to the wave of nationalism Africa had begun to experience, the Bantustans would "be geographically based on the old tribal boundaries ... North and South Sotho, Swazi, Tsonga, Tswana, Venda, Xhosa and Zulu."[78]

The full implementation of the plan, Verwoerd suggested, could take more than a century. Establishing the Bantustans involved the construction of "etho-national" states, as articulated in the Promotion of Bantu Self-Government Act.[79] The Verwoerd regime envisioned setting up purportedly independent homelands, moving to ensure that the residents would be denied political rights inside South Africa. In addition, the government hoped to speed up the division of the country into segregated regions, white and black.

Verwoerd foresaw a South African Commonwealth, which would include the High Commission territories of Basutoland, Bechuanaland, and Swaziland. Verwoerd believed that the arbitrarily constructed territories would also "become Bantustans, perhaps even with boundaries adjusted to mesh with South African reserves on their borders," according to Rodney Davenport and Christopher Saunders.[80]

By the summer of 1959, a series of violent confrontations involving blacks and South African police ensued, beginning in Durban but spreading into other sections of Natal. A number of factors precipitated the clashes, including long-standing grievances, the expropriation of African territory, the forced labor of women, and the Bantustan policy. Eventually, hundreds of black women (the men tended to be working some distance from the sites of the disturbances) endured arrest, incarceration, or dispersal by armed police. In the face of mounting social tensions, Prime Minister Verwoerd, on January 20, 1960, informed the South African parliament that a whites-only referendum would be conducted that year to determine whether the nation should become a republic. Within two years, British prime minister Harold Macmillan visited South Africa, speaking to parliament on February 3 about the "Winds of Change" sweeping through the continent. Macmillan underscored the unpopularity of South African apartheid with the British government. Quickly responding, Verwoerd pointed to the need to safeguard the rights of minority whites in Africa. South Africa, Verwoerd indicated, was a "true White state" that sought to afford blacks full rights in lands where their ancestors had resided. As for the whites, whom Verwoed insisted had enriched the continent, "We have nowhere else to go," he concluded.[81]

From the late 1940s, South Africa experienced new arbitrary borders based on both territory and race and shaped by political leaders from the prosegregationist National Party. Determined to erect an apartheid system, men such as Daniel Malan,

Johannes G. Strijdom, and Hendrik F. Verwoerd encouraged the national parliament and local councils to draw boundaries that separated whites from nonwhites throughout South African society. A number of white liberals, both inside and beyond the Unionist Party, opposed the rigidly devised barriers that the Nationalists and other segregationists demanded. More strikingly, so too did nonwhites, led by groups such as the ANC, the South African Indian Congress, and the South African Coloured People's Congress, with a general resort to nonviolent protest. More militant action occurred too, although it remained largely spontaneous and undirected.

Opposition to apartheid also arose outside South Africa, becoming particularly pronounced in both the United Nations and Great Britain, which watched unhappily as the segregationist state moved to establish black homelands, disfranchise nonwhites, view greedily the High Commission Territories, and prosecute political dissidents. Thus, the question remained whether South Africa could maintain its new system of arbitrary borders, buttressed and exemplified by apartheid.

9

A System
in Crisis

Following the Sharpeville Massacre in March 1960 (see chapter 1), the South African government continued cementing its policy of apartheid while also choosing to depart from the British Commonwealth. Thus white South African leaders proved determined to discard the arbitrary borders associated with the Commonwealth while strengthening those involving relations between white and nonwhites in South Africa. Moreover, the South African government sought to adopt a go-it-alone approach, notwithstanding surging anger at home, mounting international pressure, and the wave of nationalism sweeping across the African continent and throughout much of the globe.

Eventually, pressures would ironically mount from both the United States and the Soviet Union, chief adversaries during the Cold War, against apartheid. The new republic responded by seeking to revise its own arbitrary borders, both territorially and racially, through the speeding up of the conversion of black homelands into independent states. Hardly satisfied, black protest erupted in places like Soweto, leading to another series of catalytic events in the life of South Africa, which increasingly was being treated as a pariah by other nation-states.

In the aftermath of the tragedies related to the Sharpeville events, tensions remained high in various sectors of South Africa. Prime Minister H.F. Verwoerd continued to champion apartheid, hearkening back to 300 years earlier when both whites and blacks had come upon a "practically empty country." The whites rightfully owned the portion they had developed, and promised to defend it against any antagonists, Verwoerd insisted. The prime minister also believed that white supremacy guaranteed "survival and full development, politically and economically, to each of the other racial groups as well." He saw white leaders and those from the black homelands coming together "on a basis of absolute equality," which would result in "no discrimination and no domination." Verwoerd opposed the possibility of affording mixed nonwhite people representation in parliament, warning that would encourage "integration, 'even biological integration.'"[82]

The South African government, which, on May 31, 1961, proclaimed a republic with a new racially restrictive constitution, proceeded to crack down on political dissidents. Various ANC and PAC leaders had abandoned nonviolent approaches for those involving the selective employment of force. Many within the organizations had opposed this change in strategy, which occurred as Chief Albert Luthuli received the 1961 Nobel Peace Prize. Nevertheless, ANC and PAC members, who included whites and nonwhites in their ranks, established Umkhonto Wesizwe, an armed faction, to serve as a military wing of the resistance movement. By late 1961, Umkhonto Wesizwe resorted to acts of sabotage, targeting key economic and political installations. Shortly thereafter, two other underground groups appeared: Poqo, affiliated with the PAC, and the National Liberation Committee, connected to the ANC.

Operating on a series of different levels, the ANC sent Nelson Mandela on travels throughout Africa, where he sought support from the new, independent African states. Indeed, British authorities had steadily turned over the reins of power to nationalist parties in Africa, which joined to form the Organization of African Unity (OAU). The OAU failed to include South Africa, and called for all nations to sever diplomatic relations with the apartheid state. The United Nations, on November 6, 1962, passed a resolution imposing sanctions on South Africa. This move, which delighted Mandela, suggested an attempt by the international federation to employ economic arbitrary borders to help bring an end to South Africa's system of apartheid.

All the while, the South African government, having suffered an assassination attempt against Prime Minister Verwoerd, moved to crush the resistance movements, effectively doing so by mid-1963. The police and prosecutors targeted key figures, eventually garnering life sentences for individuals like Mandela and Walter Sisulu, both of whom were sent off to Robben Island, which held political prisoners of the apartheid regime. The government also achieved greater stability as the economy improved, thereby augmenting the appeal of the National Party. Still, for many supporters of the government, which sought to attract European immigrants, it needed to resolve the racial conundrum that afflicted South Africa. One approach involved restricting the number of Africans who dwelled in urban centers, a move opposed by both employers' organizations and trade unions.

Like the Strijdom government, Verwoerd's envisioned greater economic diversity that would permit "the Reserves to house the 'surplus' black population of the white urban areas and the white farms."[83] Thus, Verwoerd, who had agreed to limited self-government for blacks in the Transkei, attempted to begin to implement the Tomlinson Report (see chapter 8) but discovered by 1964 that greater public involvement was required. Consequently, the government offered more tax incentives, helped construct factories, and provided exemptions from labor standards. Still, too few jobs proved forthcoming as projections indicated that the size of the black population, which had more than doubled between 1911 and 1951, would continue to soar.

Piet Cillie, longtime editor of the *Die Burger*, the Cape Town Afrikaans daily newspaper, produced an important essay in 1964 titled, "Back to Our Belief in Freedom," which appeared to support Verwoerd's policy regarding the homelands. He too spoke of setting aside large blocks of territory where blacks would freely govern themselves. Moreover, blacks, along with other nonwhites, would be included within "our own nationhood in a way that does not mean their permanent subordination."

However, Cillie also warned, "The Afrikaners ought to be the last to oppose in principle the idea of national freedom and liquidation of colonialism. They inaugurated the century of anti-colonialism with their freedom struggle against British colonialism and set an example to colonized peoples throughout the world." Unfortunately, Cillie continued, "We have rejected domination over us but we did not reject our domination of other peoples as equally despicable." This had to end, he insisted:

South Africans and other non-Europeans demonstrate outside the hotel of Dag Hammarskjold, Secretary-General of the United Nations, in 1961. Hammarskjold was in Pretoria for talks with Prime Minister Hendrik Verwoerd on South Africa's racial policy. The protests followed years of violent demonstrations (and UN sanctions) against the apartheid policies of the South African government. Even British Prime Minister Harold Macmillan commented in 1962 on "the winds of change ... [and] the strength of [the] national consciousness."

"We can and should not become the last bastion of a wrong order when the Afrikaners as a people had been forged in resisting a similar order .... Old-fashioned colonialist [white] supremacy made it impossible for Afrikaners to live with themselves in good conscience because it violated their own best principles."[84]

In January 1965, the rigid Bantu Laws Amendment Act became effective, allowing the government to strip Africans, supposedly being granted independence in tribal homelands, of their already meager political rights in white regions. The seven million blacks residing outside Bantustans became "temporary dwellers" in those lands.[85] By contrast, owing to concerns about the size of the white population, the government changed residency requirements, allowing European immigrants to become citizens after only one year in South Africa, not the five years normally required. Great Britain continued to make changes of its own regarding the region, enabling the protectorate of Basutoland to become self-governing.

Verwoerd's hard-line regime ended in 1966, when another assassination attempt proved successful. The new prime minister, Balthazar J. Vorster, hardly appeared more promising to opponents of apartheid. Jailed during World War II because of his pro-Nazi stance, Vorster, as the minister of justice, had dealt with the uneasy situation following the Sharpeville massacre by allowing detention without trial. Still, as head of state, he proved more flexible than his predecessor in dealing with the new African nations. At the same time, Vorster continued Verwoerd's policy of trading with the segregationist government of Ian Smith of Rhodesia, which had recently declared its independence from Great Britain and experienced an international embargo.

Great Britain continued to grant independence to African territories, with Bechuanaland becoming the sovereign state of Botswana and Basutoland achieving its independence as Lesotho. On October 27, 1966, the UN General Assembly ended South Africa's mandate to administer South West Africa, a resolution Vorster denounced as illegal. While ignoring that proclamation, Vorster moved to establish diplomatic relations with Malawi on January 1, 1968, an action that was denounced by various members of the prime minister's own National Party as weakening apartheid. Later that year, Great Britain also granted independence to Swaziland.

The South African government subsequently acknowledged that it would not incorporate the former British protectorates, thus discarding the idea of expanding arbitrary borders through

LESOTHO AND SWAZILAND

Ringed by South African territory, both Lesotho and Swaziland received their independence from Great Britain during the last half of the 1960s. Together, these land-locked enclaves represent ideal examples of arbitrary borders. Unquestionably, the two lands repeatedly experienced the carving out of artificial boundaries that involved white settlers, various African kingdoms, and European empires. Ultimately, both achieved independence after lengthy periods of control by Great Britain. Basotho peoples settled in beautiful, mountainous Lesotho around the sixteenth century, forming small chiefdoms, cultivating territory, herding cattle, and engaging in the trade of grain, hides, and iron.

In the early stages of the nineteenth century, white traders and then Voortrekkers arrived in Basotholand, which also soon suffered the difaqane, or forced migration, of many Africans. King Moeshoeshoe the Great, who welcomed Catholic missionaries to help stave off British and Boer expansion, enabled southern Basotho society to survive, with the population of Basotholand surpassing 150,000 in 1870, the year of his death. By that point, Great Britain had annexed Basotholand, which sought protection against the Boers. As a British protectorate, Basotholand was not directly affected by the creation of the Union of South Africa. By the 1950s, the Basotholand National Council sought greater internal self-government, achieving full independence in 1966.

During the middle of the eighteenth century, the Dlamini monarch Ngwane II guided his people into southern Swaziland and the upper portion of Kwa ZuluNatal. In the 1820s, the Zulus drove the Swazis, a Bantu people, to Swaziland. Swazi king Mswazi employed military and diplomatic skills to unify the kingdom, which appeared secure by the end of his reign in 1868. However, growing numbers of European farmers had begun pouring into Swaziland, resulting in the loss of considerable portions of land. The Pretoria Convention 1881 took more territory while supposedly guaranteeing the small state's independence. During the 1880s, white prospectors discovered gold there, soon acquiring general control of Swaziland's valuable mineral resources.

The British and Boers continued making encroachments on Swaziland, which became a British protectorate following the Anglo-Boer War of 1899–1902. Led by King Sobhuza II, Swaziland fought to regain its autonomy and territory, with large amounts of land reacquired even prior to the attainment of independence in 1968.

the creation of a greater South Africa. Significantly, those newly independent states provided a safe haven for resistance movements. On the other hand, the continued holding of Angola and Mozambique as Portuguese colonies and the existence of Ian Smith's regime in Rhodesia helped establish "a *cordon sanitaire* against the infection of independence fever."[86]

Notwithstanding dissension within his own ranks, Vorster proceeded to strengthen the existing system of segregation in various ways. In late January 1968, the government, relying on the Group Areas Act (1961), removed more than 12,000 Africans from a whites-only area in northern Natal. The next month, parliament agreed to the Prohibition of Mixed Marriages Amendment Act, which deemed null and void a marriage performed abroad between a male South African and a nonwhite woman. That spring, the Separate Representation of Voters Amendment Bill continued to allow whites, chosen by the "Coloureds" to serve as their parliamentary representatives (such representation would end in 1971). The Coloured Persons' Representative Council Amendment Bill called for affording "Coloureds" their own representation, following the end of their involvement with the South African parliament. The Prohibition of Political Interference Bill sought to outlaw multiracial political organizations; this resulted in the disbanding of the multiracial Liberal Party, while leaders of the Progressive Party indicated it would henceforth exclude nonwhites.

Nevertheless, Chris Alden suggests that "the first crack in the heretofore impenetrable front presented by Afrikanerdom to the world since coming to power occurred in 1969."[87] Vorster attempted to convince conservative members of parliament that apartheid was hardly sacrosanct, that instead what was essential was "the retention, maintenance and the immortalization of Afrikaner identify within a white sovereign state." Referring to apartheid, Vorster emphasized, "If there are other better methods of achieving this end we must find those methods and get on with it."[88] Concerned about South Africa's exclusion from international sporting events, Vorster indicated that Africans from other nations would be allowed to compete in South Africa and African diplomats would be graciously received. This ironically involved a reversal of earlier, racially based arbitrary borders set by the apartheid regime.

That development, along with Vorster's assurances to English speakers that they were welcomed in the National Party, led Albert Hertzog to form the far-right-wing *Herstigte* (Refounded) National Party. The schism took place even though Vorster's government continued strengthening apartheid regulations. In February 1970, the Bantu Homelands Citizenship Bill required all Africans to become citizens of various tribal homelands, even if they did not reside there. In April, general elections, with only whites casting votes, saw Vorster's National Party remain in power, but the United Party captured nine additional parliamentary seats. Provincial elections in October 1970 produced more setbacks for the National Party.

The following January, the Polaroid Corporation added a different kind of pressure, calling for an improvement in the treatment of nonwhite employees in South Africa and condemning apartheid. In early 1972, a strike by miners in Namibia (largely situated on high plateau terrain in southern Africa, bordered by Angola and Zambia to the north, Botswana to the east, and South Africa to the south) proved damaging to the regional economy and resulted in a number of fatalities following confrontations with the police.

Undoubtedly influenced by world opinion, Vorster proceeded with plans to accord four Bantu homelands a degree of autonomy, in addition to renaming them. At mid-year, Bophuthatswana, the former Tswanaland, achieved self-government. In early August, Ciskei did as well, inducing African leaders to call for black homelands to be fitted together to create a black state. Lebowa soon became another self-governing homeland, as did Venda and Gazankulu, by January 1973. Strikes continued to ripple across South Africa, ranging from Natal to Johannesburg, resulting in improved, but still discriminatory, wages for black workers.

In early 1974, various factions within the opposition United Party demonstrated a willingness to contest apartheid policies. A number of city councils, including those in Johannesburg, Durban, and Cape Town, indicated that supposedly minor segregation practices would end in parks, libraries, and various other public places. This change in policy, which Prime Minister Vorster opposed, undoubtedly resulted from labor shortages. Notwithstanding his continued support for apartheid, Vorster did meet with leaders from the black homelands to discuss pass laws, taxes, and wage disparities, among other issues.

In October 1974, the prime minister admitted that "South Africa has come to the crossroads," and the failure to resolve matters peacefully would prove "too ghastly to contemplate." In November, Vorster also hinted that large changes were in store, stating, "Give South Africa six months ... and you will be surprised where South Africa stands then."[89] More blacks began to perform skilled work and the wages of nonwhites rose, along with social service benefits. Vorster employed still more conciliatory rhetoric, declaring, "We have a duty to Africa ... Africa is our mother ... We are Africans. We are of Africa and to my last day in politics I will strive to have us accepted by the people of Africa."[90]

In a stunning turn of events for white South Africans, colonial control of Mozambique and Angola officially ended in 1975, shortly following a coup by radical members of the Portuguese military. The termination of Portuguese hegemony ensured that "Black Africa would now be at the doorstep of the Republic." No longer did "white buffer states" stand to South Africa's north, but instead there now existed a Marxist-Leninist regime in Mozambique and a guerrilla war in Angola.[91] Pressured by Minister of Defense P.W. Botha, and hoping to end his country's diplomatic isolation, Vorster committed Defense Force troops to oppose the Soviet-backed Movimento Popular de Libertacao de Angola (MPLA). However, as American backing of opposition forces lessened, and shortly following the OAU's recognition of the MPLA regime, the South African government withdrew its troops. Fearful of a Soviet threat, Vorster now paid little attention to reforming his own country.

Back home and after a period of tranquility and apparent stability, Africans proved more determined to participate in political activity. This culminated in the sharpest spate of violence South Africa had endured in several years. Township revolts began in Soweto on June 16, 1976, when the Soweto Students' Representative Council spearheaded a march by 20,000 schoolchildren protesting an edict that Afrikaans be one of the languages employed in black schools. Most accounts indicate that the students appeared to be "good-humored, high-spirited, and excited." Some offered "the clenched-fist 'Black Power' salute," while other sported signs reading "'Down with Afrikaans,' 'We are not Boers,' and 'If we must do Afrikaans, Vorster must do Zulu.'"[92] Taunted by the students, the police hurled tear gas and then fired into the crowd, killing several. Demonstrations, strikes, and riots—with mixed nonwhites actively participating—swept across the country during the next 12 months, resulting in as many as 1,000 deaths. Thousands more went into exile, where they supported the liberation struggle.

The ANC, initially taken aback by the upheaval, attempted to take advantage of the unrest, which was fed, at least in part, by the ideology of black consciousness. Beginning in the late 1960s, a growing number of African students, led by the charismatic Stephen Biko, pored over the writings of Julius Nyerere, militant black Americans, and, above all else, the Algerian psychiatrist and revolutionary theoretician Frantz Fanon, who wrote about the cathartic nature of national liberation movements. By the early 1970s, black consciousness dug deeper roots in the townships, particularly among university students, who were attracted to the idea of "psychological emancipation."[93]

The movement gathered support from black schools at all levels while becoming subject to government persecution. Activists experienced harassment, the banning of their organizations, exile, or imprisonment. Biko initially was banned, which restricted his movement, compelled him to report regularly to

Steve Biko, a political prisoner who died at the hands of South African police
in September 1977. Biko, a charismatic speaker who helped awaken the black
consciousness, advocated "psychological emancipation" for blacks in South
Africa. Severely beaten by police until he slipped into a coma, Biko received
no medical care but instead remained naked and shackled while being shipped
to Pretoria. He died as a result of the abuse, becoming a martyr to the
liberation movement.

the police, and prevented him from engaging in political activity. Severely beaten while in police custody, the 30-year-old Biko
was battered senseless until he slipped into a coma, received no

medical care, and then remained naked and shackled while being shipped to Pretoria. As a result of the abusive treatment, he died in September 1977, becoming a martyr to the liberation movement. The government responded to an impassioned outcry following Biko's death by banning other individuals and black consciousness organizations.

Notwithstanding the increasingly volatile situation, the Nationalist Party continued to win electoral victories, obliterating the Unionists in 1977 and enabling Vorster to claim a mandate for apartheid policies. However, the so-called information scandal, involving a secret fund used to conduct psychological-political warfare to influence top figures in leading democratic nations, led to Vorster's replacement as prime minister by P.W. Botha in November 1978. Botha, who had to contend with a worsening economic situation, recognized that the system of apartheid would have to be transformed. As he indicated, Afrikaners "must adapt or die." South Africa required "rapid, visible change: the replacing of outdated political principles, the restructuring of race relations, the rejection of racial domination, the removal of humiliating discrimination and injustice, equal opportunity and rights, fewer restrictions—and a new disposition."[94]

At the same time, Botha feared that South Africa was confronting a battle between "the powers of chaos, Marxism and destruction … and the powers of order, Christian civilization and the upliftment of the people."[95] Thus, in contrast to his predecessor, Botha accepted an earlier Defense Department proposal for a "total strategy" and adopted a more aggressive stance toward Zimbabwe (the former Rhodesia), Mozambique, and Angola, with their guerrilla movements or Marxist regimes.[96]

As a new decade opened, South Africa remained the only nation on the continent with the descendents of a European settler government ruling over nonwhites. Feeling increasingly besieged after the transfer of power in Rhodesia-Zimbabwe to the black majority, the South African government backed dissident groups in neighboring states, hoping to destabilize radical regimes, including the new one in Zimbabwe under Robert Mugabe. The South African military also bombed ANC sanctuaries in Matola, Maputo, and Maseru.

Halting efforts at reform alienated far-right members of the National Party, who were expelled from the organization in 1982; led by Andries Treurnicht, they subsequently formed the Conservative Party, which championed long-standing apartheid policies. Botha also confronted the worst labor unrest in decades, when 75,000 black miners, distressed about sharply reduced wages, rioted near Johannesburg in July 1982. Seeking to address mounting racial difficulties, the prime minister called for a tricameral parliament, which would feature white, mixed nonwhite, and Asian representatives sitting in separate chambers, while blacks would continue to be excluded. Botha also sought strengthened power as head of state, with a new title of president.

In May 1983, the level of violence escalated when a car bomb killed 19, including blacks, most of whom were civilians walking outside the headquarters of the South African Air Force, located in Pretoria. Top ANC figures disagreed about the morality of this latest action, with Oliver Tambo indicating, "Never again are our people going to be doing all the bleeding," but Mandela decried the loss of civilian lives.[97] In early August, the United Democratic Front (UDF), made up of labor, community, religious, and other organizations, emerged, welcoming all opponents of apartheid. Allan Boesak, a nonwhite Dutch Reformed minister, told a gathered throng of 1,000 delegates, "We want all our rights and we want them here and we want them now." In the fashion of Martin Luther King, Jr., Boesak lifted eloquent language from the prophet Amos in declaring, "We shall not be satisfied until justice rolls down like a waterfall and righteousness like a mighty stream." Boesak envisioned "the day when all South African children will embrace each other and sing with new meaning: *Nkosi Sikelel' iAfrika*! (God Bless Africa)."[98] Among the supporters of the UDF were Albertina Sisulu, wife of the incarcerated Walter Sisulu; Mandela; and white antiapartheid leaders Helen Joseph and Beyers Naude.

In mid-1984, violence erupted in Tumahole, a black township located in the Orange Free State, with over 1,000 young people contesting rent increases and a bump in the sales tax. Now, for the first time, angry Africans targeted blacks viewed as collaborating with white officials. To the chagrin of many, the government sent military forces into Johannesburg and Cape Town to help the police. Violent protests occurred in late August following elections for the new tricameral legislature that excluded blacks. Shortly thereafter, Botha, who had recently signed a nonaggression pact with Mozambique's president Samora Machel, became South Africa's executive state president; Botha included nonwhite members in his cabinet. In October, the black Anglican bishop Desmond Tutu, a supporter of the ANC, received the Nobel Peace Prize for having waged a nonviolent struggle against apartheid.

However, both the level of violence and government repression escalated, with 70,000 troops entering the townships in early 1985, and a national state of emergency declared in June 1986. South Africa also confronted more sanctions demanded by antiapartheid activists, as well as disinvestment campaigns. The U.S. Congress itself supported sanctions against additional investments, loans, landing rights at airports, and oil exports. Botha soon terminated the pass laws, legalized black labor unions, discarded minor apartheid restrictions, and eventually accepted Namibian independence. His government, over the span of the next 12 months, also detained over 25,000 people, while the Civil Cooperation Bureau, linked to military intelligence, began to carry out acts of arson, bombings, and assassinations of left-wing figures. Nevertheless, by 1987, Botha allowed secret talks to take place with ANC representatives.

The ANC, for its part, adopted a new approach early in 1988, putting out "Constitutional Guidelines for a Democratic Society." That document, reflecting the adoption by Soviet premier Mikhail Gorbachev of the principles of *perestroika* (rebuilding) and *demokratizatsiia*, recast the Freedom Charter and lauded multiparty democracy, political liberties, and a mixed economy. The Soviet Union was in the throes of dramatic transformation of its own, which would eventually recast arbitrary borders within that giant state as well as in Eastern Europe and worldwide in the political, ideological, and territorial realms. South Africa hardly proved immune to those sweeping alterations.

Meanwhile, Joe Slovo, one of the top ANC figures and a communist activist who remained the head of Umkhonto Wesizwe, continued to support armed struggle. Still, in 1988, Botha allowed top government officials to begin conversations with the still jailed Nelson Mandela.

South Africa had come far in the late twentieth century. The 1960s opened with the Sharpeville massacre, resulting in the banning of the ANC and the PAC and leading many anti-apartheid activists to opt for armed struggle to overthrow arbitrary barriers of a racial character. Heavy-handed tactics and economic prosperity helped to quell the crisis of legitimacy that South Africa experienced, emboldening its white leaders to strengthen apartheid measures.

However, the emergence on the continent of more black-dominated nations, including some guided by Marxist-Leninist ideology and supported by the Soviet Union, coupled with the black consciousness movement, spurred greater opposition and led to new bouts of violence by the mid-1970s. South African regimes increasingly felt compelled to attempt certain compromises involving cultural, political, and racial arbitrary barriers; successive governments granted greater autonomy to the homelands and discarded various segregationist mandates.

However, in the 1980s, the ANC adopted a new, more militant position, employing sometimes terrorist tactics, which led the government to respond with greater repression. South African leader P.W. Botha sought to retain white autocracy by loosening color-based restrictions, while the ANC and other opponents of racially restrictive policies were divided as to the kinds of tactics to employ against the still-entrenched system of apartheid.

10

The New
South Africa

The crisis experienced by South Africa only intensified as the 1980s neared a close. Illness drove an increasingly irascible P.W. Botha out of office, resulting in a takeover by F.W. de Klerk, a longtime Nationalist politician but still something of an unknown quantity. Quickly, de Klerk decided it was necessary to lift various arbitrary borders of a political nature, to legalize opposition parties, including the ANC, and to release Nelson Mandela from prison. In 1994, the seemingly unimaginable occurred: Mandela became president of South Africa, ushering in a new era in international politics and bringing about the disintegration of the apartheid state and, along with it, certain racially based arbitrary borders. Consequently, South Africa possessed the potential to become a genuinely democratic, multiracial society, the majority of whose people had willingly discarded the artificial boundaries associated with apartheid.

The stroke that Botha suffered in early February 1989 and resistance to his autocratic governance led the National Party to compel his resignation that August. This occurred only weeks after Botha had met with Mandela at the presidential palace in Cape Town, and followed the beginning of a broad campaign of civil disobedience targeting segregation in hospitals, beaches, and public transportation. Violence broke out as general elections occurred in September, the results of which weakened the National Party's electoral majority.

Botha's successor, de Klerk, indicated that the election demonstrated public support for the party's plan to reform the existing system of apartheid. The next month, the government released several key political prisoners, including the ANC's Walter Sisulu, opened South Africa's beaches to all, and promised the impending abolition of the Separate Amenities Act. De Klerk also indicated that the three-year-old National Security Management System, which afforded extraordinary powers to the police and military, would be dissolved. In December 1989, de Klerk spoke directly with Mandela.

The following February, to the dismay of conservative whites, the South African president legalized the Communist Party and the PAC, ended most news censorship, and freed Mandela. Departing from prison, Mandela asserted that "the apartheid destruction on our subcontinent is incalculable," having destroyed millions of family lives, rendered millions homeless and unemployed, shattered the economy, and produced great political strife. Calling for negotiations, Mandela envisioned "a democratic, nonracial, and unitary South Africa," along with the termination of white political monopoly and economic dominance in order to address "the inequalities of apartheid."[99]

By late 1991, most of the legal edifice of apartheid, with its racially rooted arbitrary borders, crumbled altogether, while the government, the ANC, and the Inkatha Freedom Party agreed to a National Peace Accord. Those signing the document hoped to diminish the mounting level of political violence, including internecine warfare between the ANC and Chief Mangosuthu Gatsha Buthelezi's Inkatha Party (representing the nationalist sentiments of the Zulus), attacks on white civilians by the left-wing Azanian People's Liberation Army, or vigilante action by right-wing paramilitary forces.

On December 20, 1991, the Convention for a Democratic South Africa (CODESA) convened close to the Johannesburg airport to produce a new constitution and set the stage for a multiracial government. The last whites-only referendum, held in March 1992, encouraged de Klerk to proceed with negotiations. To pressure the government, the ANC waged a campaign to help oust Bantustan leaders antagonistic to the organization.

The next year witnessed both setbacks and progress. Racial tensions were heightened in the wake of the assassination on April 10, 1992, of Chris Hani of the ANC and the Communist Party. In May, the government conducted a sweep, leading to the arrest of 200 members of the PAC. However, Mandela also began negotiating with right-wing forces, including General Constand Viljoen, who headed the Afrikaner People's Front, a coalition of white groups, and Viljoen's twin brother, Bram. In October, Mandela and de Klerk received word that they were going to

Archbishop Desmond Tutu, appointed by President Nelson Mandela as head of the Truth and Reconciliation Commission in November 1995. The commission, comprising seven blacks, six whites, two mixed nonwhites, and two Indians, sought to uncover and document human rights abuses perpetrated by the South African apartheid system of government. Tutu won the Nobel Peace Prize in 1984 for his nonviolent fight against apartheid as General Secretary of the South African Council of Churches.

jointly receive the Nobel Peace Prize, and the United Nations removed most sanctions against South Africa. On November 18, negotiators agreed to an interim constitution intended to foster a democratic society, absent arbitrary barriers of a racial cast—another example of an ironic reversal of long-standing practices in the African state.

In late April 1994, the first national election under the new governing instrument produced a sweeping victory for the ANC and Mandela, who became president of South Africa. The ANC's triumph ended the last bastion of white supremacy on the continent. Nevertheless, Mandela praised his predecessor as "a first-class gentleman" and established a coalition government that included several cabinet members from the Nationalist and Inkatha Freedom parties.[100] South Africa also rejoined the British Commonwealth, with its new leaders obviously hoping to obtain preferred access to British markets, and it joined the Non-Aligned Movement. In the end, apartheid had economically crippled South Africa, particularly its nonwhites: South Africa's five million whites controlled nearly 90 percent of the land and earned nearly ten times as much as blacks.

Perhaps most important of all, President Mandela considered it essential for South Africans to address their violent history. Should the terrible deeds committed during the apartheid era remain unexamined, Mandela warned, they would "live with us like a festering sore." Demonstrating a firm desire to overcome the arbitrary barriers associated with racism, segregation, and apartheid, Mandela named a Truth and Reconciliation Commission (TRC), on November 29, 1995. Reflecting the transformed nature of South African society, the commission, headed by Archbishop Desmond Tutu, included seven blacks, six whites, two mixed nonwhites, and two Indians.

Tutu expressed hope "that we may have the strength to listen to the whispers of the abandoned, the pleas of those afraid, the anguish of those without hope."[101] The TRC included the Committee on Human Rights Violations, the Committee on Amnesty, and the Committee on Reparation and Rehabilitation. Hoping to learn from the past, the Human Rights Violation Committee, pressured by de Klerk, promised amnesty for politically motivated offenses, for which full disclosure was offered.

Over the span of two years, commissioners heard the stories of thousands of individuals who had suffered grave abuses throughout the era of apartheid, and received 22,000 victim statements. Commissioners listened to tales of terrible beatings, torture, killings, and racially drawn scientific experiments. By late 1996, the TRC concentrated more fully on perpetrators of human rights abuses, including those involved with high-level assassinations, such as the killers of Steve Biko and Chris Hani. Commission members conducted regional hearings in both

1996 and 1997, seeking to discover the redress sought by victims. The commission received amnesty applications until midnight, May 10, 1997; 7,700 were submitted.

NELSON MANDELA

Born on June 14, 1918, Rolihlahla Nelson Dalbhunga Mandela was the son of a Thembu chief in the Transkei. Educated at a missionary school in Healdtown, Mandela heard a Xhosa poet foresee eventual independence for South Africa. While studying at Fort Hare University, Mandela met Oliver Tambo and joined him in a student strike that resulted in their suspension.

Serving as a law clerk in Johannesburg in the 1940s, Mandela undertook legal studies through the University of Witwatersrand. In 1943, he joined a bus boycott in Alexandra contesting fare increases. The next year, Mandela, along with Tambo and Walter Sisulu, helped to found the African National Congress Youth League. That organization devised a program of action supporting nonviolent economic boycotts, strikes, and demonstrations. Along with Tambo, Mandela also opened Africa's first black legal firm, although he devoted the bulk of his attention to political activity.

In 1952, Mandela helped to kick off the ANC's Defiance Campaign against unjust laws. The government responded by banning him. Increasingly distressed by the ANC's nonmilitant stance, Mandela proved instrumental in the group's adoption in 1955 of the Freedom Charter, which insisted that South Africa belonged to all of its residents.

Following the Sharpeville Massacre in March 1960, Mandela helped to establish the Umkhonto Wesizwe, or Spear of the Nation movement, which initiated a campaign involving sabotage and guerrilla activity. ANC leaders went underground in 1961, with Mandela acquiring the reputation as a "Black Pimpernel," long able to avoid the Bureau of State Security forces.

Tried but acquitted in the infamous Treason Trial of that period, Mandela suffered another arrest and prosecution in 1962, resulting in his lengthy incarceration on Robben Island. While behind bars, he read widely, learned Afrikaans, and attempted to maintain the spirits of his fellow prisoners. Fourteen years later, Mandela refused a reduced sentence in return for his acknowledgment of the legitimacy of the Transkei homeland government.

No individual proved more instrumental in the establishment of the TRC than President Mandela, referred to by Tutu as "an icon of forgiveness." Explaining his desire to demonstrate

Nevertheless, he increasingly believed that compromise was necessary. As Mandela recalled, "We had right on our side, but not yet might. It was clear to me that a military victory was a distant if not impossible dream. It simply did not make sense for both sides to lose thousands if not millions of lives in a conflict that was unnecessary.... It was time to talk."*

As his reputation continued to grow, Mandela, along with several other prisoners, was transferred in 1982 to Pollsmoor Prison outside Cape Town. Six years later, he was diagnosed with tuberculosis and then moved to Victor Verster Prison Farm. By this point, he stood as "the world's most famous political prisoner."** Secret negotiations took place with government officials, leading to the unconditional release from jail in early 1990 of Mandela, now 71 years old and gray-haired, but still tall and elegant.

Notwithstanding his 27 years in prison, Mandela demonstrated a firm commitment to democracy, racial equality for all peoples, and majority rule. In 1993, Mandela shared the Nobel Peace Prize with South African president F.W. de Klerk, whom he replaced in office after general elections in May 1994. Three years later, Mandela ceded the ANC presidency to Thabo Mbeki, who followed him into office in 1999. Graca Machel, the widow of Samora Machel, the former president of Mozambique, discussed the impact of her husband (they married in 1998, the day he turned 80 years old) on South Africa. As Machel saw matters, Mandela

> "symbolizes a much broader forgiveness and understanding and reaching out. If he had come out of prison and sent a different message, I can tell you this country could be in flames.... He knew exactly the way he wanted to come out, but also the way he addressed the people from the beginning, sending the message of what he thought was the best way to save lives in this country to bring reconciliation...."****

* Quoted in Graybill, *Truth and Reconciliation in South Africa*, p. 17.

** Quoted in Eades, *The End of Apartheid in South Africa*, p. 136.

*** Quoted in Sampson, *Mandela*, p. 525.

magnanimity, Mandela declared, "I could not wish what happened to me and my people on anyone." For his part, Tutu remained disappointed that white leaders failed to acknowledge that they had possessed "an evil system" and now demanded forgiveness "without qualification."[102] The admission of guilt, Tutu believed, was necessary so that South Africa could move forward. As he explained during an early session of the TRC,

> We are charged to unearth the truth about our dark past, and to lay the ghosts of that past so that they will not return to haunt us; and that we will thereby contribute to the healing of the traumatized and wounded—for all of us in South Africa are wounded people.[103]

Not everyone was pleased with the hearings, and many nonwhites condemned the notion of amnesty for terrible crimes, while whites, led by the National Party, viewed some of the proceedings as amounting to a witch hunt. An African woman, whose husband had been murdered, warned, "No government can forgive. No commission can forgive. Only I can forgive. And I am not ready to forgive."[104] Accusations also mounted that favoritism was displayed to the ANC, but Mandela himself resigned from the organization in 1997. Clashes occurred with former presidents Botha and de Klerk; having refused to testify, Botha suffered a contempt citation, along with a suspended jail sentence, while de Klerk considered himself besmirched by allegations of human rights violations. Eventually, Tutu felt compelled to apologize to de Klerk, who had withdrawn from both the government and the committee proceedings. The refusal to grant amnesty in various instances, such as to the murderers of Biko and Hani, angered many Afrikaners and led to charges of bias.

In accepting the commission's final report, Mandela acknowledged on October 29, 1998, that "the wounds of the period of repression and resistance are too deep to have been healed by the TRC alone, however well it has encouraged us along that path." Still, he continued, "the report that today becomes the property of our nation should be a call to all of us to celebrate and to strengthen what we have done as a nation as we leave our terrible past behind us forever."[105]

The commission's anticipated findings displeased Botha, de Klerk, and the ANC. The commission indicated that "Botha contributed to and facilitated a climate in which ... gross violations of human rights could and did occur, and as such is accountable for such violations." Charged with covering up bombings, de Klerk went to court to have such findings suppressed.

The ANC similarly sought an injunction to prevent the release of the commission's report. An angry Tutu condemned the ANC's "abuse of power" and warned, "Yesterday's oppressed can quite easily become today's oppressors.... We've seen it happen all over the world and we shouldn't be surprised if it happens here."[106]

Referring to the commission, Pulitzer Prize–winning author Tina Rosenberg suggests, "No institution for dealing with the past anywhere in the world has taken on as ambitious a portfolio."[1087] After including this quote from Rosenberg in the preface to her own book, *Truth and Reconciliation in South Africa*, Lyn S. Graybill acknowledged that "the TRC was certainly not perfect by any means. It was a compromise between the morally ideal and the politically possible." Still, Graybill suggests that "nations moving through democratic transitions may indeed find a workable model in South Africa's ethical yet pragmatic experiment in dealing with the past." As Graybill notes, Elizabeth Kiss also considers the TRC "an 'especially promising tool' in places such as eastern and central Europe, Northern Ireland, and the Middle East, where there are violators and perpetrators on multiple sides."[108]

Guided by Nelson Mandela, a longtime political-prisoner-turned-head-of-state, South Africa in the mid-1990s discarded the arbitrary borders of a racial, cultural, and political nature associated with discriminatory practices, segregation, and apartheid. While convinced that his nation must remember the wrongs connected with those barriers, Mandela also firmly believed that old and recent grievances had to be shed as fully as

Nelson Mandela, ANC leader and longtime foe of apartheid, several days after his release in 1990, after 27 years in prison. Mandela went on to share the Nobel Peace Prize with F.W. de Klerk in 1992 and to be elected as president of South Africa in April 1994. He was the first nonwhite ruler in the country's history.

possible to enable South Africa to move beyond its troubled past. He envisioned a democratic, racially diverse South Africa capable of healing old wounds and of reconstructing a new nation, where arbitrary borders rooted in racial prejudices, hatreds, and fears would be discarded.

Indeed, Mandela hoped that the new South Africa would become a model for a free, pluralistic society that had deliberately chosen the path of reconciliation, notwithstanding centuries of poisonous and exploitative arbitrary borders of a racial cast. Certainly the South Africa Mandela helped to usher in again underscored the illusory quality of artificial frontiers that sought to maintain white hegemony in the midst of demands by nonwhite majorities for an end to racially restrictive practices.

2200 B.C. San hunter-gatherers and Khoikhoi hunter-gatherers are present in Southern Africa.

300 A.D. Brown-skinned people, speaking Bantu languages, migrate south of the Limpopo River.

1300–1500 The Khoisan control the southern and southwestern Cape territory.

Portuguese sailors begin sailing around the Cape on the way to India.

1650s Dutch East India Company establishes a post at the Cape of Good Hope. Slaves arrive at the Cape. Fighting occurs between the Dutch and Khoikhoi.

1650s
Dutch East India Company establishes a post at the Cape of Good Hope; slaves arrive at the Cape. Fighting occurs between the Dutch and Khoikhoi

1870s
Great Britain annexes the South African Republic and the Orange Free State

1806
The Second British invasion begins, along with reoccupation

1911
Union of South Africa is established

1650s

1911

1820–1830s
Great Treks occur

1690s
Trekboers head into the Cape interior

1899–1902
South African War takes place

1690s	Trekboers head into the Cape interior.
1779	Initial Cape-Xhosa frontier war takes place.
1795	British begin to occupy the Cape.
1806	Second British invasion starts, along with reoccupation.
1816	Zulu kingdom conducts Mfeqane in southern Africa.
1820s–1830s	Great Treks occur.
1845	Great Britain annexes Natal.
1850s	Boers create the republics of the South African Republic and the Orange Free State.
1868–1870s	Great Britain annexes Basutoland, the South African Republic, and the Orange Free State.
1880–1881	Transvaal Boers conduct war of independence.

1913
Segregation laws begin

1962
Several ANC leaders, including Nelson Mandela and Walter Sisulu, receive sentences of life imprisonment

1994
Mandela is elected president

1949
National Party wins the general elections, promising a program of apartheid

1912

1996

1912
South African Native National Congress (renamed the African National Congress in 1923) is formed

1960
Sharpeville Massacre occurs

1996
Truth and Reconciliation Commission begins hearings

1976
Soweto uprisings take place

1899–1902	South African War takes place.
1910	Union of South Africa is established.
1912	South African Native National Congress (renamed the African National Congress in 1923) is formed.
1913	Segregation laws begin.
1948	National Party wins the general elections, promising a program of apartheid.
1956	ANC issues Freedom Charter.
1959	Pan Africanist Congress is formed.
1960	Sharpeville Massacre occurs.
1962	Several ANC leaders, including Nelson Mandela and Walter Sisulu, receive sentences of life imprisonment.
1976	Soweto uprisings take place.
1982	Conservative Party breaks away from National Party.
1990	Mandela is released from prison.
1994	Mandela is elected president.
1996	Truth and Reconciliation Commission begins hearings.

Chapter 1

1. Quoted in John Reader, *Africa: A Biography of the Continent*. New York: Vintage, 1999, p. 666.
2. Quoted in Kathryn A. Manzo, *Domination, Resistance, and Social Change in South Africa*. Westport, Connecticut: Praeger, 1992, p. 187.
3. Ibid., p. 188.
4. Quoted in Harold Macmillan, "Winds of Change" address to the South African parliament, February 3, 1960.
5. Quoted in Ambrose Reeves, *Shooting at Sharpeville: The Agony of South Africa*. Boston: Houghton Mifflin, 1961, p. 36.
6. Quoted in Robert Maja, "Documentary II: Extracts from Evidence before the Court of Enquiry," in *Shooting at Sharpeville*, p. 89.
7. Quoted in Reeves, *Shooting at Sharpeville*, p. 38.
8. Quoted in Elias Lelia, "Documentary II," p. 135.
9. Quoted in Reeves, *Shooting at Sharpeville*, pp. 41–43.
10. Ibid., p. 44.
11. Quoted in Frank Welsh, *South Africa: A Narrative History*. New York: Kodansha International, 1999, p. 454.
12. Quoted in Motsoko Pheko, *Apartheid: The Story of a Dispossessed People*. London: Marram Books, 1984, p. 99.
13. Quoted in Allister Sparks, *The Mind of South Africa*. New York: Alfred A. Knopf, 1990, p. 235.

Chapter 2

14. Quoted in Manzo, *Domination, Resistance, and Social Change in South Africa*, p. 35.
15. Ibid., pp. 36–37.
16. Quoted in Timothy Keegan, *Colonial South Africa and the Origins of the Racial Order*. Charlottesville: University Press of Virginia, 1996, p. 22.
17. Quoted in Leonard Thompson, *A History of South Africa*. New Haven: Yale University Press, 2001, pp. 44–45.
18. Quoted in Keegan, *Colonial South Africa and the Origins of the Racial Order*, p. 21.
19. Quoted in Simon Richmond, et al., *South Africa, Lesotho and Swaziland*.

Melbourne: Lonely Planet Publications, 2001, p. 20.
20. Quoted in Robert Ross, *A Concise History of South Africa*. Cambridge: Cambridge University Press, 1999, p. 26.
21. Quoted in Nigel Worden, *The Making of Modern South Africa*. Oxford: Blackwell, 1995, p. 10.
22. Quoted in Reader, *Africa*, p. 463.
23. Quoted in Keegan, *Colonial South Africa and the Origins of the Racial Order*, p. 126.
24. Quoted in Ross, *A Concise History of South Africa*, p. 38.
25. Quoted in Welsh, *South Africa*, p. 136.

Chapter 3

26. Ibid., p. 139.
27. Quoted in Thompson, *A History of South Africa*, p. 86.
28. Quoted in Welsh, *South Africa*, p. 140.
29. Ibid., South Africa, p. 109.
30. Quoted in Ross, *A Concise History of South Africa*, p. 36.
31. Quoted in Thompson, *A History of South Africa*, p. 88.
32. Ibid., p. 93.
33. Ibid., p. 95.
34. Quoted in Welsh, *South Africa*, p. 210.
35. Quoted in Keegan, *Colonial South Africa and the Origins of the Racial Order*, p. 207.

Chapter 4

36. Quoted in Welsh, *South Africa*, p. 213.
37. Ibid.
38. Ibid.
39. Quoted in Manzo, *Domination, Resistance, and Social Change in South Africa*, pp. 42–43.
40. Quoted in Thompson, *A History of South Africa*, p. 117.
41. Quoted in Worden, *The Making of Modern South Africa*, p. 19.
42. Quoted in John Reader, *Africa: A Biography of the Continent*. New York, Vintage Books, 1999, p. 497.

Chapter 5

43. Ibid., p. 515.
44. Quoted in Welsh, *South Africa*, p. 271.

45. Ibid., pp. 272–273.
46. Quoted in Rodney Davenport and Christopher Saunders, *South Africa: A Modern History*. London: Macmillan Press, 2000, p. 210.
47. Quoted in Worden, *The Making of Modern South Africa*, p. 24.
48. Quoted in J.M. Roberts, *The Penguin History of the World*. London: Penguin Books, 1997, p. 778.
49. Quoted in Thompson, *A History of South Africa*, p. 121.
50. Quoted in Reader, *Africa*, p. 520.
51. Quoted in Thompson, *A History of South Africa*, p. 138.
52. Ibid., p. 141.
53. Quoted in Bill Nasson, *The South African War, 1899–1902*. London: Arnold, 1999, p. 7.
54. Ibid., p. 230.
55. Ibid., p. 231.

Chapter 6

56. Quoted in Welsh, *South Africa*, pp. 361–362.
57. Quoted in Blaine T. Browne and Robert C. Cottrell, *Uncertain Order: The World in the Twentieth Century*. Upper Saddle River, New Jersey: Prentice-Hall, 2003, p. 140.
58. Quoted in Davenport and Saunders, *South Africa*, p. 263.
59. Quoted in Thompson, *A History of South Africa*, p. 153.
60. Quoted in Ross, *A Concise History of South Africa*, p. 83.
61. Quoted in Thompson, *A History of South Africa*, p. 157.

Chapter 7

62. Ibid., p. 175.
63. Quoted in Welsh, *South Africa*, pp. 384–385.
64. Quoted in Manzo, *Domination, Resistance, and Social Change in South Africa*, p. 56.
65. Quoted in Davenport and Saunders, *South Africa*, pp. 302–303.
66. Ibid., pp. 307, 309–310.
67. Quoted in Welsh, *South Africa*, p. 403.
68. Quoted in Davenport and Saunders, *South Africa*, p. 335.

69. Quoted in Thompson, *A History of South Africa*, p. 171.
70. Quoted in Davenport and Saunders, *South Africa*, p. 344.
71. Quoted in Thompson, *A History of South Africa*, p. 182.
72. Quoted in Davenport and Saunders, *South Africa*, p. 361.

Chapter 8

73. Ibid., p. 370.
74. Quoted in Eileen Riley, *Major Political Events in South Africa, 1948–1970*. Oxford: Facts on File, 1991, p. 11.
75. Ibid., p. 28.
76. Quoted in Thompson, *A History of South Africa*, p. 191.
77. Ibid., p. 208.
78. Quoted in Riley, *Major Political Events in South Africa, 1948–1990*, p. 61.
79. Quoted in Welsh, *South Africa*, p. 449.
80. Quoted in Davenport and Saunders, *South Africa*, p. 408.
81. Quoted in Riley, *Major Political Events in South Africa, 1948–1990*, p. 67.
82. Quoted in Hermann Giliomee, *The Afrikaners: Biography of a People*. Charlottesville: University of Virginia Press, 2003, pp. 521, 526.

Chapter 9

83. Quoted in Davenport and Saunders, *South Africa*, p. 425.
84. Quoted in Giliomee, *The Afrikaners*, pp. 530–531.
85. Quoted in Riley, *Major Political Events in South Africa, 1948–1990*, p. 90.
86. Quoted in Chris Alden, *Apartheid's Last Stand: The Rise and Fall of the South African Security State*. Macmillan Press, 1996, p. 19.
87. Ibid., p. 20.
88. Quoted in Giliomee, *The Afrikaners*, p. 557.
89. Ibid., p. 565.
90. Ibid., p. 567.
91. Alden, *Apartheid's Last Stand*, p. 23.
92. Quoted in Giliomee, *The Afrikaners*, p. 579.
93. Quoted in Sparks, *The Mind of South Africa*, p. 263.

94. Quoted in Welsh, *South Africa*, p. 479.
95. Ibid.
96. Quoted in William Gutteridge, "South Africa: Strategy for Survival?" in *South Africa: From Apartheid to National Unity, 1981–1994*, ed. by Gutteridge. Aldershot, England: Dartmouth, 1995, p. 2.
97. Quoted in Riley, *Major Political Events in South Africa, 1948–1990*, p. 183.
98. Quoted in Steven Mufson, *Fighting Years: Black Resistance and the Struggle for a New South Africa*. Boston: Beacon Press, 1990, p. 48.
99. Quoted in Nelson Mandela, "Speech by Nelson Mandela in Cape Town Following His Release from Prison, February 11, 1990," in Lindsay Michie Eades, *The End of Apartheid in South Africa*. Westport, Connecticut: Greenwood Press, 1999, pp. 170–171.

Chapter 10

100. Quoted in Patti Waldmeir, *Anatomy of a Miracle: The End of Apartheid and the Birth of the New South Africa*. New York: W.W. Norton & Company, 1997, p. 39.
101. Quoted in Martin Meredith, *Coming to Terms: South Africa's Search for Truth*. New York: Public Affairs, 1999, pp. 18, 25.
102. Quoted in Lyn S. Graybill, *Truth and Reconciliation in South Africa: Miracle or Model?* Boulder, Colorado: Lynne Rienner Publishers, 2002, p. 11, 21, 42.
103. Quoted in Meredith, *Coming to Terms*, p. 3.
104. Quoted in Eades, *The End of Apartheid in South Africa*, p. 111.
105. Quoted in Dorothy C. Shea, *The South African Truth Commission: The Politics of Reconciliation*. Washington, D.C.: United States Institute of Peace Press, 2000, p. 3.
106. Quoted in Anthony Sampson, *Mandela: The Authorized Biography*. New York: Vintage Books, 2001, p. 523.
107. Quoted in Tina Rosenberg, "Foreword," p. x, in *Coming to Terms*.
108. Quoted in Graybill, *Truth and Reconciliation in South Africa*, pp. 177–179.

Davenport, Rodney, and Christopher Saunders. *South Africa: A Modern History.* London: Macmillan Press, 2000.

Eades, Lindsay Michie. *The End of Apartheid in South Africa.* Westport, Connecticut: Greenwood Press, 1999.

Giliomee, Hermann. *The Afrikaners: Biography of a People.* Charlottesville: University of Virginia Press, 2003.

Graybill, Lyn S. *Truth and Reconciliation in South Africa: Miracle or Model?* Boulder, Colorado: Lynne Rienner Publishers, 2002.

Gutteridge, William. "South Africa: Strategy for Survival?" in *South Africa: From Apartheid to National Unity, 1981–1994*, ed. by Wm. Gutteridge. Aldershot, England: Dartmouth, 1995.

Keegan, Timothy. *Colonial South Africa and the Origins of the Racial Order.* Charlottesville: University of Virginia Press, 1996.

Lelia, Elias. "Documentary II: Extracts from Evidence Before the Court of Enquiry," in *Shooting at Sharpeville: The Agony of South Africa.* Boston: Houghton Mifflin, 1961.

Maja, Robert. "Documentary II: Extracts from Evidence Before the Court of Enquiry," in *Shooting at Sharpeville.*

Mandela, Nelson. "Speech by Nelson Mandela in Cape Town Following His Release from Prison, February 11, 1990," in *The End of Apartheid in South Africa*, by Lindsay Michie Eades. Westport, Connecticut: Greenwood Press, 1999.

Manzo, Kathryn A. *Domination, Resistance, and Social Change in South Africa.* Westport, Connecticut: Praeger, 1992.

Meredith, Martin. *Coming to Terms: South Africa's Search for Truth.* New York: Public Affairs, 1999.

Mufson, Steven. *Fighting Years: Black Resistance and the Struggle for a New South Africa.* Boston: Beacon Press, 1990.

Nasson, Bill. *The South African War, 1899–1902.* London: Arnold, 1999.

Pheko, Motsoko. *Apartheid: The Story of a Dispossessed People*. London: Marram Books, 1984.

Reader, John. *Africa: A Biography of the Continent*. New York: Vintage Books, 1999.

Reeves, Ambrose. *Shooting at Sharpeville: The Agony of South Africa*. Boston: Houghton Mifflin, 1961

Richmond, Simon, et al. *South Africa, Lesotho and Swaziland*. Melbourne: Lonely Planet Publications, 2001.

Riley, Eileen. *Major Political Events in South Africa, 1948–1970*. Oxford: Facts on File, 1991.

Roberts, J.M. *The Penguin History of the World*. London: Penguin Books, 1997.

Ross, Robert. *A Concise History of South Africa*. Cambridge: Cambridge University, 1999.

Sampson, Anthony. *Mandela: The Authorized Biography*. New York: Vintage Books, 2000.

Saunders, Christopher, and Nicholas Southey. *Historical Dictionary of South Africa*, 2nd edition. Lanham, Maryland: Scarecrow Press, 2000.

Shea, Dorothy C. *The South African Truth Commission: The Politics of Reconciliation*. Washington, D.C.: United States Institute of Peace Press, 2000.

Sparks, Allister. *The Mind of South Africa*. New York: Alfred A. Knopf, 1990.

Thompson, Leonard. *A History of South Africa*. New Haven:Yale University Press, 2001.

Waldmeir, Patti. *Anatomy of a Miracle: The End of Apartheid and the Birth of the New South Africa*. New York: W.W. Norton & Company, 1997.

Welsh, Frank. *South Africa: A Narrative History.* New York: Kodansha International, 1999.

Worden, Nigel. *The Making of Modern South Africa.* Oxford: Blackwell, 1995.

Ballinger, Margaret. *From Union to Apartheid: A Trek to Isolation.* Cape Town: Juta, 1969.

Beinart, William. *Twentieth-Century South Africa.* New York: Oxford University Press, 1994.

Bhana, Surendra. *Gandhi's Legacy: The Natal Indian Congress, 1894–1994.* Pietermaritzburg: University of Natal Press, 1997.

Dubow, Saul. *Racial Segregation and the Origins of Apartheid in South Africa, 1919–1936.* Basingstoke: Macmillan, 1989.

Ellis, Stephen, and Tsepo Sechaba. *Comrades Against Apartheid: The ANC and the South African Communist Party in Exile.* Bloomington: Indiana University Press, 1992.

Elphick, Richard, and Hermann Giliomee. *The Shaping of South African Society, 1652–1840.* Cape Town: Maskew Miller Longman, 1989.

Frederickson, George M. *Black Liberation: A Comparative History of Black Ideologies in the United States and South Africa.* New York: Oxford University Press, 1995.

———. *White Supremacy: A Comparative Study in American and South African History.* New York: Oxford University Press, 1981.

Gerhart, Gail M. *Black Power in South Africa: The Evolution of an Ideology.* Berkeley: University of California Press, 1979.

Hall, Martin. *The Changing Past: Farmers, Kings and Traders in Southern Africa, 200–1860.* Cape Town: David Philip, 1987.

Haysom, Nicholas. *Mabangalana: The Rise of Right-Wing Vigilantes in South Africa.* Johannesburg: University of the Witwatersrand, Centre for Applied Legal Studies, 1986.

Holland, Heidi. *The Struggle: A History of the African National Congress.* London: Grafton, 1989.

Kirk, Thandeka Joyce F. *Making a Voice: African Resistance to Segregation in South Africa.* Boulder, Colorado: Westview Press, 1998.

Lazerson, Joshua N. *Against the Tide: Whites in the Struggle Against Apartheid.* Boulder, Colorado: Westview Press, 1994.

Liebenberg, Ian, et al. *The Long March.* Cape Town: HAUM, 1994.

Lobban, Michael. *White Man's Justice: South African Political Trials in the Black Consciousness Era.* Oxford: Clarendon Press, 1996.

Lyon, Peter. "The Old Commonwealth: The First Four Dominions" in *The Oxford History of the Twentieth Century,* eds. Michael Howard and Wm. Roger Louis. New York: Oxford University Press, 2000.

Mandela, Nelson. *Long Walk to Freedom.* Boston: Little, Brown, 1994.

Moodie, T. Dunbar, and Vivienne Ndatshe. *Going for Gold: Men, Mines, and Migration.* Johannesburg: Witwatersrand University Press, 1994.

Mostert, Noel. *Frontiers: The Epic of South Africa's Creation and the Tragedy of the Xhosa People.* London: Cape, 1992.

O'Meara, Dan. *Forty Lost Years: The Apartheid State and the Politics of the National Party, 1948–1994.* Johannesburg: Ravan, 1995.

Plaatje, Solomon Tshekisho. *Native Life in South Africa.* Johannesburg: Ravan, 1995.

Price, Robert M. *The Apartheid State in Crisis: Political Transformation in South Africa, 1975–1990.* New York: Oxford University Press, 1991.

Rich, Paul B. *White Power and the Liberal Conscience: Racial Segregation and South African Liberalism, 1921–60.* Johannesburg: Ravan Press, 1984.

Stedman, Stephen J., ed. *South Africa: The Political Economy of Transformation.* Boulder, Colorado: Lynne Rienner, 1994.

Thompson, Leonard. *The Unification of South Africa, 1902–1910.* Oxford: Clarendon Press, 1960.

page:

7: ©Bettman/CORBIS
15: Library of Congress, LC-USZC4-2069
18: ©Hulton-Deutsch Collection/CORBIS
30: ©Gideon Mendel/CORBIS
43: Library of Congress, LC-USZ62-40653
52: Library of Congress, LC-DIG-ggbain-00058
56: Library of Congress, LC-USZ62-90969
64: ©Hulton-Deutsch Collection/CORBIS

73: ©Bettman/CORBIS
80: Library of Congress, LC-USW33-022635-C
92: ©Louise Gubb/CORBIS SABA
99: ©Hulton-Deutsch Collection/CORBIS
106: Associated Press, AP
114: Associated Press, AP
120: Associated Press, AP

frontis: © MAPS.com/CORBIS

Robert C. Cottrell, Professor of History and American Studies at California State University, Chico, is the author of many books, including *Izzy: A Biography of I. F. Stone, Roger Nash Baldwin and the American Civil Liberties Union, The Best Pitcher in Baseball: The Life of Rube Foster, Negro League Giant,* and *Uncertain Order: The World in the Twentieth Century.* Named the Outstanding Professor at CSUC in 1998, Professor Cottrell received the 2000 Wang Family Excellence Award for Social & Behavioral Sciences & Public Services, a system-wide honor for the 23 campuses that make up the California State University.

George J. Mitchell served as chairman of the peace negotiations in Northern Ireland during the 1990s. Under his leadership, an historic accord, ending decades of conflict, was agreed to by the governments of Ireland and the United Kingdom and the political parties in Northern Ireland. In May 1998, the agreement was overwhelmingly endorsed by a referendum of the voters of Ireland, North and South. Senator Mitchell's leadership earned him worldwide praise and a Nobel Peace Prize nomination. He accepted his appointment to the U.S. Senate in 1980. After leaving the Senate, Senator Mitchell joined the Washington, D.C. law firm of Piper Rudnick, where he now practices law. Senator Mitchell's life and career have embodied a deep commitment to public service and he continues to be active in worldwide peace and disarmament efforts.

James I. Matray is professor of history and chair at California State University, Chico. He has published more than forty articles and book chapters on U.S.-Korean relations during and after World War II. Author of *The Reluctant Crusade: American Foreign Policy in Korea, 1941–1950* and *Japan's Emergence as a Global Power,* his most recent publication is *East Asia and the United States: An Encyclopledia of Relations Since 1784.* Matray also is international columnist for the *Donga libo* in South Korea.